AN AMERICAN ORIGINAL

Cream cheese was developed over 100 years ago and was first produced commercially by an ambitious, hard-working farmer in upstate New York. It was primarily used as a flavorful spread for bread, toast or crackers. Fresh fruit preserves were added to this delightful new cheese giving it a novel taste-twist and creating an almost endless variety of sandwiches and snacks.

This fresh, delicate, creamy-smooth cheese was not used as a recipe ingredient until the mid 1920's. One of the first recipes developed was the "Kraft Philadelphia Cream Cake," which was later retitled "Supreme Cheesecake." Although versions of this original recipe appear in this magazine, it was first published in a 1928 Kraft recipe folder and became an instant favorite.

In the late 1940's and early 50's, America discovered cocktail parties and casual home entertaining. Certainly this new life-style helped give birth to appetizers, finger sandwiches and cream cheese dips. These food innovations were so popular that when "Clam Appetizer Dip" was originally featured on the Kraft Music Hall television show, New York City was sold out of canned clams within 24 hours.

We've come a long way from that first "Kraft Philadelphia Cream Cake." The simple cheesecake has matured and grown and become far more glamorous as we marble it with chocolate, top it with meringues, garnish it with kiwi fruit, flavor it with everything from peanut butter to liqueurs.

Today, we've even found a way to make a lighter style of cream cheese with 25% less fat and 20% fewer calories. It's called *Light* PHILADELPHIA BRAND Neufchâtel Cheese. It's similar in taste and texture to regular cream cheese and is superb when used in your favorite cream cheese recipes.

What began as a novel idea—cooking with cream cheese—has become a universally accepted concept. Today, PHILADELPHIA BRAND Cream Cheese is an indispensable ingredient used by great American cooks, like you.

AN AMERICAN FAVORITE

PHILADELPHIA BRAND Cream Cheese spread on bread, toast, crackers or bagels has always been one of the most popular uses for this most popular product. Today, with *Soft* PHILADELPHIA BRAND Cream Cheese, it's even easier.

Soft "Philly" Cream Cheese is made with the same wholesome ingredients as traditional cream cheese. The fresh, delicate flavor is the same. Significantly different is the consistency which is what makes Soft "Philly" Cream Cheese completely spreadable, even when taken directly from the refrigerator.

Although it was developed and is most often used as a spreading cheese, Soft "Philly" Cream Cheese is suitable for many recipes. You'll especially like it for recipes that require blending with chilled ingredients such as when you're making dips, spreads, frostings, cold sauces or fillings. In recipes designating regular cream cheese, soft cream cheese should not be substituted because a softer consistency may result.

Soft "Philly" Cream Cheese is always ready. Whether you need to quickly satisfy a hungry youngster home from school—or you need to magically make attractive and tasty appetizers suddenly appear for unexpected guests—Soft "Philly" Cream Cheese is the quick and easy answer.

You'll find a number of recipes within this magazine created especially for Soft PHILADELPHIA BRAND Cream Cheese. Many can be prepared with a minimum of effort and others are more elegant ideas for parties and special entertaining.

GREAT BEGINNINGS

PARTY CHEESE BALL

2 8-oz. pkgs. PHILADELPHIA
   BRAND Cream Cheese,
   softened
2 cups (8 ozs.) shredded
   CRACKER BARREL Brand
   Sharp Natural Cheddar
   Cheese
1 tablespoon chopped pimento
1 tablespoon chopped green
   pepper
1 tablespoon finely chopped
   onion
2 teaspoons worcestershire
   sauce
1 teaspoon lemon juice
   Dash of ground red pepper
   Dash of salt
   Chopped pecans

Combine cream cheese and cheddar
cheese, mixing at medium speed on
electric mixer until well blended. Add all
remaining ingredients except pecans;
mix well. Chill several hours. Shape into
ball; roll in pecans. Serve with crackers.

Approximately 2 cups

VARIATIONS

■ Omit pecans. Roll in finely chopped
parsley, dried beef or toasted chopped
almonds.

■ Shape into log. Coat top and bottom
of log with chopped parsley. Slice; serve
with crackers or cucumber slices.

■ Shape into 1-inch balls. Roll in
chopped nuts, dried beef, toasted
sesame seed or chopped parsley.

■ Shape into pyramid. Coat one side
with chopped nuts, second side with
chopped parsley and third side with
chopped dried beef. Serve with party
rye bread.

■ Shape into football; coat with pecans.
Top with pimento strips to form lacing.

Top: Dill Dip (see page 8)
Bottom: Party Cheese Ball

DILL DIP

1 8-oz. pkg. *Light*
   PHILADELPHIA BRAND
   Neufchâtel Cheese,
   softened
1/2 cup KRAFT Light Reduced
   Calorie Mayonnaise
3 tablespoons milk
1/4 cup chopped green onion
1 tablespoon chopped parsley
3/4 teaspoon dill weed
1/4 teaspoon celery salt
1/4 teaspoon onion powder

Combine neufchâtel cheese, mayonnaise and milk, mixing until well blended. Stir in remaining ingredients. Chill. Serve with vegetable dippers.

1 1/2 cups

SAUSAGE IN PASTRY

1 8-oz. pkg. PHILADELPHIA
   BRAND Cream Cheese,
   softened
1 cup PARKAY Margarine
2 cups flour
1 lb. smoked sausage, cut into
   1/2-inch pieces

Combine cream cheese and margarine, mixing at medium speed on electric mixer until well blended. Add flour; mix well. Shape into ball; chill. Divide pastry in half. On lightly floured surface, roll each pastry half to 12 × 15-inch rectangle; cut into 3-inch squares. Place sausage piece in center of each pastry square. Bring edges together, pressing to seal. Place on cookie sheet. Bake at 400°, 20 minutes. Serve with SAUCEWORKS Hot Mustard Sauce.

Approximately 40 appetizers

QUICK MEXICAN SPREAD

1 8-oz. pkg. *Light*
   PHILADELPHIA BRAND
   Neufchâtel Cheese,
   softened
1 4-oz. can chopped green
   chilies, drained

Combine neufchâtel cheese and chilies, mixing until well blended; chill. Serve with tortilla chips or spread over warm tortillas or corn bread.

1 cup

CURRIED CHICKEN PUFFS

½ cup water
⅓ cup PARKAY Margarine
⅔ cup flour
Dash of salt
2 eggs

* * *

1 8-oz. pkg. PHILADELPHIA
BRAND Cream Cheese,
softened
¼ cup milk
¼ teaspoon salt
Dash of curry powder
Dash of pepper
1½ cups chopped cooked
chicken
⅓ cup slivered almonds,
toasted
2 tablespoons green onion
slices

Bring water and margarine to boil. Add flour and salt; stir vigorously over low heat until mixture forms ball. Remove from heat; add eggs, one at a time, beating until smooth after each addition. Place level measuring tablespoonfuls of batter on ungreased cookie sheet. Bake at 400°, 25 minutes. Cool.

Combine cream cheese, milk, salt, curry powder and pepper, mixing until well blended. Add chicken, almonds and onions; mix lightly. Cut tops from cream puffs; fill with chicken mixture. Replace tops. Place puffs on cookie sheet. Bake at 375°, 5 minutes or until warm.

Approximately 1½ dozen

NOTE
Unfilled cream puffs can be prepared several weeks in advance and frozen. Place puffs on a jelly roll pan and wrap securely in moisture-vaporproof wrap.

Curried Chicken Puffs

CLAM APPETIZER DIP

1 8-oz. can minced clams
1 8-oz. pkg. PHILADELPHIA
   BRAND Cream Cheese,
   softened
2 teaspoons lemon juice
1½ teaspoons worcestershire
   sauce
¼ teaspoon garlic salt
   Dash of pepper

Drain clams, reserving ¼ cup liquid. Combine clams, reserved liquid and remaining ingredients, mixing until well blended. Chill. Serve with potato chips or vegetable dippers.

1½ cups

CREAMY GINGER DIP

1 8-oz. pkg. *Light*
   PHILADELPHIA BRAND
   Neufchâtel Cheese,
   softened
2 tablespoons orange juice
2 tablespoons KRAFT Orange
   Marmalade
⅛ teaspoon ground ginger
   Assorted fresh fruit

Combine ingredients, mixing until well blended. Chill. Serve with fruit.

1 cup

SERVING SUGGESTION
For a breakfast treat, serve Creamy Ginger Dip with fruit muffins or nut bread.

Creamy Ginger Dip

hilly" Stuffed Mushrooms

PHILLY" STUFFED MUSHROOMS ▬▬▬

2 lbs. medium mushrooms
6 tablespoons PARKAY Margarine
1 8-oz. pkg. PHILADELPHIA BRAND Cream Cheese, softened
1/2 cup (2 ozs.) crumbled KRAFT Natural Blue Cheese
2 tablespoons chopped onion

Remove mushroom stems; chop enough stems to measure 1/2 cup. Cook half of mushroom caps in 3 tablespoons margarine over medium heat, 5 minutes; drain. Repeat with remaining mushroom caps and margarine. Combine cream cheese and blue cheese, mixing until well blended. Stir in chopped stems and onions; fill mushroom caps. Place on cookie sheet; broil until golden brown.

Approximately 2 1/2 dozen

ZUCCHINI CHIVE DIP

1 8-oz. container Soft
   PHILADELPHIA BRAND
   Cream Cheese
3 tablespoons milk
1 small zucchini, shredded
3 tablespoons chopped chives
¹/₈ teaspoon salt

Combine cream cheese and milk, mixing until well blended. Add remaining ingredients; mix well. Chill. Serve with vegetable dippers or chips.

1 cup

IMPROMPTU APPETIZER

¹/₄ cup **SAUCEWORKS** Cocktail
   Sauce
1 8-oz. pkg. **PHILADELPHIA**
   BRAND Cream Cheese
   Frozen cooked tiny shrimp,
   thawed

Pour cocktail sauce over cream cheese; top with shrimp. Serve with crackers or party rye bread slices.

VARIATIONS
Substitute any of the following for cocktail sauce and shrimp:
■ ¹/₄ cup KRAFT Horseradish Sauce mixed with 1 teaspoon KRAFT Pure Prepared Mustard and finely chopped ham.
■ 2¹/₄-oz. can deviled ham and sweet pickle relish.
■ Crisply cooked crumbled bacon and green onion slices.
■ ¹/₃ cup KRAFT Pineapple Preserves combined with ¹/₂ teaspoon KRAFT Prepared Horseradish and ¹/₂ teaspoon KRAFT Pure Prepared Mustard.
■ ¹/₄ to ¹/₃ cup chutney.
■ ¹/₄ cup picante sauce, taco sauce or salsa.

HINT
Keep the ingredients for this quick and delicious recipe on hand for impromptu parties and unexpected guests.

Top: Appetizer Pâté Cheesecake (see page 14
Middle: Zucchini Chive Di
Bottom: Impromptu Appetize

APPETIZER PÂTÉ CHEESECAKE

1 cup crushed plain croutons
3 tablespoons PARKAY
    Margarine, melted

    *   *   *

1 envelope unflavored gelatin
1/2 cup cold water
2 8-oz. pkgs. PHILADELPHIA
    BRAND Cream Cheese,
    softened
1 8-oz. pkg. braunschweiger or
    liver sausage
1/4 cup KRAFT Real
    Mayonnaise
3 tablespoons chopped
    pimento
2 tablespoons grated onion
1 tablespoon KRAFT Pure
    Prepared Mustard
1/2 teaspoon lemon juice

Combine croutons and margarine; press onto bottom of 9-inch springform pan. Bake at 350°, 10 minutes.

Soften gelatin in water; stir over low heat until dissolved. Combine cream cheese and braunschweiger, mixing at medium speed on electric mixer until well blended. Gradually add gelatin. Stir in remaining ingredients until blended; pour over crust. Chill until firm. Remove rim of pan.

16 servings

SHERRIED SPREAD

1 8-oz. pkg. PHILADELPHIA
    BRAND Cream Cheese,
    softened
1 tablespoon sherry
2 tablespoons chopped pecans

Combine cream cheese and sherry, mixing until well blended. Stir in pecans. Chill. Serve with party rye or pumpernickel bread slices.

1 cup

ZESTY HERB SPREAD

1 8-oz. pkg. *Light*
    PHILADELPHIA BRAND
    Neufchâtel Cheese,
    softened
1 tablespoon chopped chives
1/4 teaspoon dried basil leaves,
    crushed
    Dash of pepper

Combine ingredients, mixing until well blended. Chill. Serve with party rye bread slices or vegetable dippers.

1 cup

HINT
Keep a crock of Zesty Herb Spread in the refrigerator for unexpected guests or ready-to-eat snacking.

FLORENTINE DIP

1 8-oz. pkg. *Light*
   **PHILADELPHIA BRAND
   Neufchâtel Cheese,
   softened**
1/2 cup plain yogurt
2 tablespoons milk
1 10-oz. pkg. frozen spinach,
   thawed, well-drained,
   chopped
2 hard-cooked eggs, finely
   chopped
1/4 teaspoon pepper
1/4 teaspoon salt

Combine neufchâtel cheese, yogurt and milk, mixing until well blended. Stir in remaining ingredients. Serve with vegetable dippers.

2½ cups

Petite "Philly" Pinwheels

PETITE "PHILLY" PINWHEELS ━━━━━

1 8-oz. can PILLSBURY
   Refrigerated Quick
   Crescent Dinner Rolls
   Soft PHILADELPHIA
   BRAND Cream Cheese
1/2 cup finely chopped ham
2 tablespoons finely chopped
   stuffed green olives

Separate dough into four rectangles; firmly press perforations to seal. Spread with cream cheese; sprinkle with ham and olives, pressing lightly. Roll up, starting at short end; seal edges. Cut each roll into four slices. Place, cut-side down, on ungreased cookie sheet; flatten slightly. Bake at 375°, 15 to 17 minutes or until golden brown.

16 appetizers

VARIATION
■ Substitute dried apricots and green pepper for ham and olives.

GARDEN VEGETABLE SPREAD

1 8-oz. container Soft
   PHILADELPHIA BRAND
   Cream Cheese
1/2 cup shredded carrot
1/2 cup shredded zucchini
1 tablespoon chopped parsley
1/4 teaspoon garlic salt
   Dash of pepper

Combine ingredients; mix well. Chill.
Serve with party rye or pumpernickel
bread slices or assorted crackers.

1 1/3 cups

VARIATION
■ Serve with LENDER'S Pre-Sliced
Frozen Plain Bagelettes, toasted.

REFRESHING CUCUMBER DIP

1 8-oz. pkg. PHILADELPHIA
   BRAND Cream Cheese,
   softened
1/2 cup sour cream
1 tablespoon milk
1 teaspoon grated onion
1/4 teaspoon worcestershire
   sauce
1/3 cup finely chopped
   cucumber

Combine all ingredients except
cucumbers, mixing until well blended.
Stir in cucumbers. Chill several hours or
overnight. Serve with chips or vegetable
dippers.

1 2/3 cups

HOT CRABMEAT APPETIZER

1 8-oz. pkg. PHILADELPHIA
   BRAND Cream Cheese,
   softened
1 7 1/2-oz. can crabmeat,
   drained, flaked
2 tablespoons finely chopped
   onion
2 tablespoons milk
1/2 teaspoon KRAFT Cream
   Style Horseradish
1/4 teaspoon salt
   Dash of pepper
1/3 cup sliced almonds, toasted

Combine all ingredients except
almonds, mixing until well blended.
Spoon mixture into 9-inch pie plate;
sprinkle with almonds. Bake at 375°,
15 minutes. Serve with crackers.

Approximately 1 1/2 cups

VARIATIONS
■ Substitute 8-oz. can minced clams,
drained, for crabmeat.
■ Omit almonds; sprinkle with dill
weed.

HOT BEEF DIP

1/4 cup chopped onion
1 tablespoon PARKAY Margarine
1 cup milk
1 8-oz. pkg. PHILADELPHIA BRAND Cream Cheese, cubed
1 3-oz. pkg. smoked sliced beef, chopped
1 4-oz. can mushrooms, drained
1/4 cup (1 oz.) KRAFT Grated Parmesan Cheese
2 tablespoons chopped parsley

Saute onions in margarine. Add milk and cream cheese; stir over low heat until cream cheese is melted. Add remaining ingredients; heat thoroughly, stirring occasionally. Serve hot with French bread slices, if desired.

2 1/2 cups

VARIATION
■ Substitute 2 1/2-oz. pkg. smoked sliced turkey for 3-oz. pkg. smoked sliced beef.

SERVING SUGGESTION
For a colorful variety, serve with French, whole-wheat or rye bread cubes.

PINE NUT CHEESE SPREAD

1 8-oz. pkg. PHILADELPHIA BRAND Cream Cheese, softened
2 tablespoons KRAFT Grated Parmesan Cheese
1/4 cup chopped green pepper
1 tablespoon finely chopped onion
2 teaspoons chopped pimento
Dash of ground red pepper
1/3 cup pine nuts or slivered almonds, toasted

Combine all ingredients except pine nuts, mixing until well blended. Chill. Shape into log. Coat with pine nuts just before serving.

1 cup

VARIATION
■ Substitute *Light* PHILADELPHIA BRAND Neufchâtel Cheese for cream cheese. Increase parmesan cheese to 1/4 cup (1 ounce). Spoon into serving container. Top with pine nuts just before serving.

HINT
Homemade cheese spreads in colorful containers make great hostess gifts. Include the recipe for an added personal touch.

Top: Hot Beef Dip
Bottom: Pine Nut Cheese Spread

THREE WAY SPLIT SPREADS

1 8-oz. pkg. *Light*
    PHILADELPHIA BRAND
    Neufchâtel Cheese,
    softened
2 cups (8 ozs.) shredded
    100% Natural **KRAFT**
    Mild Cheddar Cheese
1/3 cup milk
2 tablespoons finely chopped
    green pepper
2 tablespoons shredded carrot
1 teaspoon grated onion
            *   *   *
2 crisply cooked bacon slices,
    crumbled
1 1/2 teaspoons **KRAFT** Prepared
    Horseradish (optional)
            *   *   *
1/4 teaspoon dill weed
1/8 teaspoon garlic powder
1/8 teaspoon pepper

Combine neufchâtel cheese, cheddar cheese and milk, mixing at medium speed on electric mixer until well blended. Divide mixture into three 2/3-cup portions. To one portion, add green peppers, carrots and onions; mix well.

To second portion, add bacon and horseradish; mix well.

To third portion, add seasonings; mix well.

Arrange cheese spreads on serving tray; serve with crackers.

2 cups

SHRIMP APPETIZER CRESCENTS

1 8-oz. pkg. *Light*
    PHILADELPHIA BRAND
    Neufchâtel Cheese,
    softened
1 cup finely chopped cooked
    shrimp
1/3 cup (1 1/2 ozs.) **KRAFT**
    Grated Parmesan Cheese
1 tablespoon milk
2 8-oz. cans **PILLSBURY**
    Refrigerated Quick
    Crescent Dinner Rolls
1 egg, beaten
1 teaspoon water

Combine neufchâtel cheese, shrimp, parmesan cheese and milk, mixing until well blended. Separate crescent dough into eight rectangles; firmly press perforations to seal. Spread each rectangle evenly with 2 rounded measuring tablespoonfuls neufchâtel cheese mixture. Cut each rectangle into six triangles; roll as directed on package. Place on greased cookie sheets; brush with combined egg and water. Bake at 375°, 12 to 15 minutes or until golden brown. Serve warm.

4 dozen

VARIATIONS
■ Substitute 6 1/2-oz. can tuna, drained, flaked for shrimp.
■ Substitute PHILADELPHIA BRAND Cream Cheese for Neufchâtel Cheese.

HERB APPETIZER CHEESECAKE

1 cup dry bread crumbs
1/4 cup PARKAY Margarine,
   melted

     *   *   *

1/4 cup olive oil
2 cups fresh basil leaves
1/2 teaspoon salt
1 garlic clove, cut in half
2 8-oz. pkgs. PHILADELPHIA
   BRAND Cream Cheese,
   softened
1 cup ricotta cheese
3 eggs
1/2 cup (2 ozs.) KRAFT Grated
   Parmesan Cheese
1/2 cup pine nuts

Combine crumbs and margarine; press onto bottom of 9-inch springform pan. Bake at 350°, 10 minutes.

Place oil, basil, salt and garlic in blender container. Cover; process on high speed until smooth. Combine basil mixture, cream cheese and ricotta cheese, mixing at medium speed on electric mixer until well blended. Add eggs, one at a time, mixing well after each addition. Blend in parmesan cheese; pour over crust. Top with pine nuts. Bake at 325°, 1 hour and 15 minutes. Loosen cake from rim of pan; cool before removing rim of pan. Serve warm or at room temperature. Garnish with tomato rose and fresh basil, if desired. Chill any remaining cheesecake.

16 servings

VARIATION
■ Substitute 1 cup chopped parsley and 1 tablespoon dried basil leaves for fresh basil leaves.

Herb Appetizer Cheesecake

Easy Appetizer Cut-Outs

EASY APPETIZER CUT-OUTS

1 15-oz. pkg. PILLSBURY All
   Ready Pie Crusts
1 8-oz. pkg. PHILADELPHIA
   BRAND Cream Cheese,
   softened
1 tablespoon milk
1/2 teaspoon onion salt
1/2 teaspoon worcestershire
   sauce
   Cucumber slices
   Chopped chives
   Dill weed
   Green onion slices
   Radish slices
   Carrot curls
   Pimento slices
   Parsley
   Cleaned small shrimp

Unfold pie crusts; cut out with 2½-inch
cutters. Place cut-outs on ungreased
cookie sheet; prick each several times
with fork. Bake at 425°, 8 to 10 minutes
or until golden brown; cool. Combine
cream cheese, milk, onion salt and
worcestershire sauce; mixing until well
blended. Spread on cut-outs; top with
remaining ingredients as desired.

2 dozen

APPETIZER PIZZA

1 7.5-oz. can PILLSBURY
  Refrigerated Buttermilk
  Biscuits
1 medium onion, cut into
  rings
1 cup chopped zucchini
1 4-oz. can mushrooms,
  drained
2 tablespoons PARKAY
  Margarine
1 8-oz. pkg. PHILADELPHIA
  BRAND Cream Cheese,
  softened
1/4 cup milk
1 egg, beaten
1/2 teaspoon salt

Separate each biscuit into two layers. Place on bottom and sides of greased 12-inch pizza pan, pressing together to form crust. Saute onions, zucchini and mushrooms in margarine. Combine cream cheese, milk, egg and salt, mixing until well blended. Stir in vegetables. Pour over crust. Bake at 400°, 20 to 25 minutes, or until crust is golden brown. Serve warm.

14 to 16 servings

SIX POINT SPREAD

1 8-oz. pkg. PHILADELPHIA
  BRAND Cream Cheese,
  softened
1 cup (4 ozs.) shredded
  KRAFT 100% Natural
  Swiss Cheese
4 crisply cooked bacon slices,
  crumbled
2 tablespoons green onion
  slices
1 teaspoon worcestershire
  sauce
2 tablespoons milk

Combine cream cheese and Swiss cheese, mixing at medium speed on electric mixer until well blended. Add remaining ingredients; mix well. Chill. Serve with assorted crackers.

1²/₃ cups

Hawaiian Coconut Dip

HAWAIIAN COCONUT SPREAD

1 8-oz. container Soft
   PHILADELPHIA BRAND
   Cream Cheese
2 tablespoons KRAFT Apricot,
   Pineapple or Peach
   Preserves
1/3 cup flaked coconut

Combine cream cheese and preserves, mixing until well blended. Add coconut; mix well. Chill. Serve with nut bread slices.

1 1/3 cups

VARIATIONS
■ Add 1/8 teaspoon anise seed.
■ Substitute 1/4 cup whole berry cranberry sauce for KRAFT Preserves.

MOLDED SHRIMP SPREAD

1 8-oz. pkg. *Light*
  PHILADELPHIA BRAND
  Neufchâtel Cheese,
  softened
1 6-oz. bag frozen cooked tiny
  shrimp, thawed, drained
¼ cup chopped pitted ripe
  olives
1 2-oz. jar sliced pimento,
  drained, chopped
2 teaspoons lemon juice
1½ teaspoons instant minced
  onion
½ teaspoon worcestershire
  sauce
½ teaspoon hot pepper sauce

Combine ingredients, mixing until well blended. Press mixture into 2-cup bowl. Chill several hours. Unmold. Serve with crackers.

2 cups

VARIATIONS
■ Substitute 6-ozs. fresh cleaned shrimp, cooked, finely chopped, for frozen shrimp.
■ Substitute PHILADELPHIA BRAND Cream Cheese for Neufchâtel Cheese.

CREAMY DEVILED EGGS

8 hard-cooked eggs
1 8-oz. container Soft
  PHILADELPHIA BRAND
  Cream Cheese
2 tablespoons sweet pickle
  relish
½ teaspoon dry mustard
¼ teaspoon salt
  Dash of pepper

Cut eggs in half. Remove yolks; mash. Blend in cream cheese, relish and seasonings, mixing until well blended. Refill whites.

16 deviled eggs

MAIN MEAL MAGIC

CREAMY FETTUCINI ALFREDO

1 8-oz. pkg. PHILADELPHIA
 BRAND Cream Cheese,
 cubed
3/4 cup (3 ozs.) KRAFT Grated
 Parmesan Cheese
1/2 cup PARKAY Margarine
1/2 cup milk
8 ozs. fettucini, cooked,
 drained

In large saucepan, combine cream
cheese, parmesan cheese, margarine
and milk; stir over low heat until
smooth. Add fettucini; toss lightly.
4 servings

"PHILLY" CHIVE SAUCE

1 8-oz. pkg. *Light*
 PHILADELPHIA BRAND
 Neufchâtel Cheese, cubed
1/2 cup milk
1 tablespoon chopped chives
1 teaspoon lemon juice
1/4 teaspoon garlic salt

Combine neufchâtel cheese and milk in
saucepan; stir over low heat until
smooth. Stir in remaining ingredients.
Serve over hot cooked potatoes, green
beans, broccoli or asparagus.
1 1/3 cups

VARIATION
■ Substitute PHILADELPHIA BRAND
Cream Cheese for Neufchâtel cheese.

Creamy Fettucini Alfredo

STUFFED SQUASH

- ¼ cup slivered almonds
- 1 tablespoon PARKAY Margarine
- 1 8-oz. pkg. *Light* PHILADELPHIA BRAND Neufchâtel Cheese, cubed
- ¾ cup milk
- 1 10-oz. pkg. frozen cut green beans, cooked, drained
- ½ cup water chestnuts, sliced
- 1½ teaspoons lemon juice
- ½ teaspoon dry mustard
- ¼ teaspoon ground ginger
- ¼ teaspoon salt
- 2 acorn squash, cut in half, baked

Saute almonds in margarine in saucepan until lightly browned. Add neufchâtel cheese and milk; stir over low heat until neufchâtel cheese is melted. Stir in all remaining ingredients except squash; heat thoroughly, stirring occasionally. Spoon vegetable mixture into hot squash.

4 servings

NOTES

To bake acorn squash: Cut squash lengthwise into halves; scoop out seeds. Place squash, cut-side down, in 13 × 9-inch baking pan. Add enough hot water to measure ½ inch up sides of pan. Bake at 375°, 45 to 55 minutes, or until squash is tender.

Prepare vegetable mixture as directed omitting squash. Spoon vegetable mixture over 4 cups hot cooked noodles.

Stuffed Squash

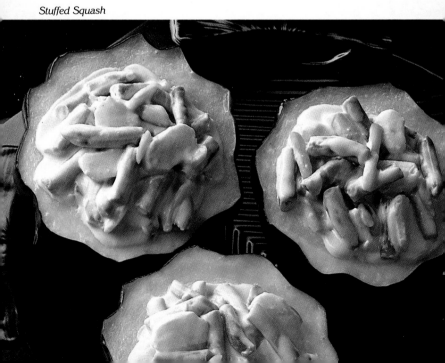

CREAMY TUNA ON BAGELS

1 8-oz. pkg. PHILADELPHIA
  BRAND Cream Cheese,
  softened
1 6½-oz. can tuna, drained,
  flaked
2 tablespoons green onion
  slices
½ teaspoon dill weed
  Dash of salt and pepper
3 LENDER'S Pre-Sliced
  Frozen Bagels, toasted

Combine all ingredients except bagels;
mix lightly. Spread bagel halves with
cream cheese mixture. Broil 5 to 7
minutes or until thoroughly heated.

6 servings

VARIATION
■ Omit salt. Substitute 6¾-oz. can
chunk ham, drained, flaked, for tuna.

CHICKEN TACOS

1 8-oz. pkg. PHILADELPHIA
  BRAND Cream Cheese,
  cubed
⅓ cup milk
1½ cups chopped cooked
  chicken
1 4-oz. can chopped green
  chilies, drained
½ teaspoon salt
¼ teaspoon chili powder or
  ground cumin
10 taco shells
  Shredded lettuce
  Chopped tomato

Combine cream cheese and milk in
saucepan; stir over low heat until
smooth. Stir in chicken, chilies and
seasonings; heat thoroughly, stirring
occasionally. Fill taco shells with meat
mixture, lettuce and tomatoes.

10 tacos

HOMESPUN SCALLOPED POTATOES

1 8-oz. pkg. PHILADELPHIA
  BRAND Cream Cheese,
  cubed
1¼ cups milk
½ teaspoon salt
⅛ teaspoon pepper
4 cups thin potato slices
2 tablespoons chopped chives

In large saucepan, combine cream
cheese, milk, salt and pepper; stir over
low heat until smooth. Add potatoes
and chives; mix lightly. Spoon into
1½-quart casserole; cover. Bake at
350°, 1 hour and 10 minutes or until
potatoes are tender. Stir before serving.

6 servings

MAKE AHEAD
Prepare as directed except for baking.
Cover; refrigerate overnight. When ready
to serve, bake as directed.

TEMPTING CHEESE CREPES

2/3 cup flour
1/2 teaspoon salt
3 eggs, beaten
1 cup milk

* * *

2 8-oz. pkgs. *Light*
PHILADELPHIA BRAND
Neufchâtel Cheese,
softened
1/4 cup sugar
1 teaspoon vanilla
Strawberry-Banana Topping

Combine flour, salt and eggs; beat until smooth. Gradually add milk, mixing until well blended. For each crepe, pour 1/4 cup batter into hot, lightly greased 8-inch skillet or crepe pan, tilting skillet to cover bottom. Cook over medium-high heat until lightly browned on both sides, turning once.

Combine neufchâtel cheese, sugar and vanilla, mixing until well blended. Spread approximately 1/4 cup neufchâtel cheese mixture onto each crepe. Fold in thirds. Place in 13×9-inch baking dish. Bake at 350°, 15 to 20 minutes or until thoroughly heated. Serve with Strawberry-Banana Topping.

8 servings

PREPARATION TIP

Lightly grease and preheat the skillet or crepe pan until a drop of water sizzles when sprinkled on. If the skillet isn't really hot, crepes may be too thick and stick to the pan.

STRAWBERRY-BANANA TOPPING

1 10-oz. pkg. frozen
strawberries, thawed
1 tablespoon cornstarch
1 banana, sliced

Drain strawberries, reserving liquid. Add enough water to reserved liquid to measure 1 1/4 cups; gradually add to cornstarch in saucepan, stirring until well blended. Bring to boil over medium heat, stirring constantly. Boil 1 minute. Stir in fruit.

2 cups

Top: "Philly" Brunch Quiche (see page 32,
Bottom: Tempting Cheese Crepes

"PHILLY" BRUNCH QUICHE ▬▬▬▬

Pastry for 1-crust 10-inch
pie
     *   *   *
1 8-oz. pkg. PHILADELPHIA
  BRAND Cream Cheese,
  cubed
1 cup milk
4 eggs, beaten
1/4 cup chopped onion
1 tablespoon PARKAY
  Margarine
1 cup finely chopped ham
1/4 cup chopped pimento
1/4 teaspoon dill weed
  Dash of pepper

On lightly floured surface, roll pastry to 12-inch circle. Place in 10-inch pie plate. Turn under edge; flute. Prick bottom and sides of pastry with fork. Bake at 400°, 12 to 15 minutes or until pastry is lightly browned.

Combine cream cheese and milk in saucepan; stir over low heat until smooth. Gradually add cream cheese mixture to eggs, mixing until well blended. Saute onions in margarine. Add onions and remaining ingredients to cream cheese mixture; mix well. Pour into pastry shell. Bake at 350°, 35 to 40 minutes or until set. Garnish with ham slices and fresh dill, if desired.

8 servings

VARIATIONS
■Substitute 1/4 cup finely chopped green pepper for dill weed.
■Substitute 10-oz. pkg. frozen chopped spinach, cooked, drained, 1 cup (4 ozs.) shredded KRAFT 100% Natural Swiss Cheese and 6 crisply cooked bacon slices, crumbled, for ham, pimento and dill weed.
■Substitute 4-oz. pkg. pepperoni slices, chopped, 1/4 cup (1 oz.) KRAFT Grated Parmesan Cheese and 1/2 teaspoon dried oregano leaves, crushed, for ham, pimento and dill weed. Place pepperoni on bottom of pastry shell; continue as directed.

Vegetable Stir-Fry

VEGETABLE STIR-FRY

1 8-oz. pkg. *Light*
 PHILADELPHIA BRAND
 Neufchâtel Cheese, cubed
¼ cup sesame seed, toasted
2 cups diagonally-cut carrot
 slices
2 cups diagonally-cut celery
 slices
¾ cup thin green pepper strips
2 tablespoons PARKAY
 Margarine
¼ teaspoon salt
 Dash of pepper

Coat neufchâtel cheese cubes with sesame seed; chill. In large skillet or wok, stir-fry vegetables in margarine and seasonings until crisp-tender. Remove from heat. Add neufchâtel cheese to vegetables; mix lightly.

6 to 8 servings

VARIATION
■ Substitute PHILADELPHIA BRAND Cream Cheese for Neufchâtel Cheese.

LAYERED CHICKEN SALAD

1 8-oz. pkg. *Light*
    PHILADELPHIA BRAND
    Neufchâtel Cheese,
    softened
2 medium avocados, peeled,
    mashed
1/4 cup milk
1 tablespoon lemon juice
1 tablespoon chopped onion
1/2 teaspoon salt
4 cups shredded lettuce
1 cup chopped red or green
    pepper
2 cups chopped cooked
    chicken
1 11-oz. can mandarin orange
    segments, drained
4 crisply cooked bacon slices,
    crumbled

Combine neufchâtel cheese, avocados, milk and juice, mixing until well blended. Add onions and salt; mix well. In 2 1/2-quart glass serving bowl, layer lettuce, peppers, chicken and oranges. Spread neufchâtel cheese mixture over salad. Cover; chill. Top with bacon just before serving.

6 to 8 servings

SHRIMP A LA PARISIENNE

2 tablespoons **PARKAY**
    Margarine, melted
1 lb. cleaned shrimp
2 cups mushroom slices
2 tablespoons green onion
    slices
1 8-oz. pkg. **PHILADELPHIA**
    BRAND Cream Cheese,
    cubed
1/4 cup milk
1/2 cup (2 ozs.) shredded 100%
    Natural **KRAFT** Swiss
    Cheese
3 tablespoons dry white wine
2 tablespoons dry bread
    crumbs

Reserve 2 teaspoons melted margarine. Saute shrimp in remaining margarine 3 to 5 minutes or until pink. Add mushrooms and onions; cook until tender. Remove shrimp and mushrooms from pan with slotted spoon; add cream cheese and milk to pan. Stir over low heat until smooth. Add Swiss cheese and wine; stir until cheese is melted. Return shrimp mixture to pan; mix lightly. Spoon into four lightly greased 4-ounce baking dishes. Combine reserved margarine and crumbs. Sprinkle over shrimp mixture. Broil 1 to 2 minutes or until golden brown.

4 servings

VARIATION

■ Substitute one 1-quart casserole for four individual baking dishes.

"PHILLY" KABOBS

2/3 cup KRAFT "Zesty" Italian
    Dressing
1 1/2 lbs. round steak, cut into
    strips
1/4 cup chopped onion
1 tablespoon PARKAY
    Margarine
1 8-oz. pkg. PHILADELPHIA
    BRAND Cream Cheese,
    cubed
3/4 cup milk
1/4 cup (1 oz.) KRAFT Grated
    Parmesan Cheese
1/4 teaspoon dry mustard
2 cups summer squash, cut
    into 1/2-inch slices
1 cup cherry tomatoes
    Hot cooked rice

Pour dressing over steak. Cover; marinate in refrigerator several hours or overnight. Drain, reserving dressing. Saute onions in margarine. Add cream cheese and milk; stir over low heat until cream cheese is melted. Stir in parmesan cheese and mustard.

Indoors
Thread steak and vegetables accordian style on skewers; place on rack of broiler pan. Broil 8 to 10 minutes or to desired doneness, brushing frequently with reserved dressing and turning occasionally. Serve over rice. Top with cream cheese mixture.

Outdoors
Thread steak and vegetables accordian style on skewers; place on greased grill over hot coals (coals will be glowing). Grill, uncovered, to desired doneness, brushing frequently with reserved dressing and turning occasionally. Serve over rice. Top with cream cheese mixture.

6 servings

CREAMY RICE PILAF

2 beef bouillon cubes
2 1/4 cups boiling water
1 cup regular long grain rice
1 cup carrot slices
2 tablespoons green onion
    slices
1 tablespoon PARKAY
    Margarine
1/2 teaspoon dill weed
1 8-oz. pkg. PHILADELPHIA
    BRAND Cream Cheese,
    cubed
2 tablespoons KRAFT Real
    Mayonnaise

Dissolve bouillon in water in saucepan; add rice, vegetables, margarine and dill weed. Cover; simmer 20 minutes or until water is absorbed and rice is tender. Remove from heat. Add cream cheese and mayonnaise; stir until cream cheese is melted.

6 servings

GARDEN MACARONI SALAD

1/4 cup KRAFT Real Mayonnaise
1 8-oz. pkg. PHILADELPHIA
BRAND Cream Cheese,
softened
1/4 cup sweet pickle relish,
drained
1 tablespoon KRAFT Pure
Prepared Mustard
2 cups (7 ozs.) elbow
macaroni, cooked, drained
1 cup chopped cucumber
1/2 cup chopped green pepper
1/2 cup radish slices
2 tablespoons chopped onion
1/2 teaspoon salt

Gradually add mayonnaise to cream cheese, mixing until well blended. Stir in relish and mustard. Add remaining ingredients; mix lightly. Spoon into lightly oiled 9-inch springform pan with ring insert. Chill several hours or overnight. Unmold. Garnish with cucumber slices and radish roses, if desired.

6 to 8 servings

VARIATION
■ Add 1/2 cup (2 ozs.) KRAFT Grated Parmesan Cheese to cream cheese mixture.

TURKEY WITH HERB SAUCE

1 pkg. (approximately
1 1/4 lbs.) fresh turkey
breast slices
1/4 cup flour
1/4 teaspoon salt
2 tablespoons oil
                *   *   *
1 8-oz. pkg. *Light*
PHILADELPHIA BRAND
Neufchâtel Cheese, cubed
1/3 cup milk
1 garlic clove, minced
1 teaspoon grated onion
1/4 teaspoon dried oregano
leaves, crushed
1/8 teaspoon pepper

Coat turkey with combined flour and salt. Cook turkey on both sides in hot oil over medium-high heat 4 to 6 minutes or until turkey loses pink color.

Combine neufchâtel cheese and milk; stir over low heat until smooth. Stir in garlic, onion and seasonings. Serve over turkey.

4 servings

Garden Macaroni Salad

FESTIVE CHICKEN SALAD

1 8¼-oz. can crushed
   pineapple, undrained
1 8-oz. container Soft
   PHILADELPHIA BRAND
   Cream Cheese
2 cups chopped cooked
   chicken
1 8-oz. can water chestnuts,
   drained, sliced
½ cup celery slices
½ cup slivered almonds,
   toasted
¼ cup green onion slices
¼ teaspoon salt
   Dash of pepper
4 medium tomatoes
   Lettuce

Drain pineapple, reserving ¼ cup liquid. Combine reserved liquid and cream cheese, mixing until well blended. Add pineapple, chicken, water chestnuts, celery, ¼ cup almonds, onions, salt and pepper; mix lightly. Chill. Cut each tomato into six wedges, almost to stem end. Fill with chicken mixture. Sprinkle with remaining almonds. Serve on lettuce-lined plates.

4 servings

VARIATIONS

■ Omit tomatoes; serve salad over honeydew or cantaloupe wedges or in lettuce cups.
■ Substitute chopped pecans for almonds.

EGG SALAD MAGNIFIQUE

1 8-oz. pkg. PHILADELPHIA
   BRAND Cream Cheese,
   softened
½ cup KRAFT Real
   Mayonnaise
1 tablespoon KRAFT Cream
   Style Prepared Horseradish
6 hard cooked eggs, chopped
1 6-oz. pkg. frozen crabmeat,
   thawed, drained
½ cup chopped celery
½ cup chopped red or green
   pepper
6 croissants, split
   Lettuce

Combine cream cheese, mayonnaise and horseradish, mixing until well blended. Add eggs, crabmeat, celery and peppers; mix lightly. Chill. Fill croissants with lettuce and egg mixture.

6 sandwiches

Festive Chicken Salad

Creamy Topped Fruit Salad

CREAMY TOPPED FRUIT SALAD ▬▬▬▬

1 8-oz. pkg. *Light*
    PHILADELPHIA BRAND
    Neufchâtel Cheese,
    softened
2 tablespoons lemon juice
1 teaspoon grated lemon peel
$1/2$ cup whipping cream
$1/4$ cup powdered sugar
2 cups peach slices
2 cups blueberries
2 cups strawberry slices
2 cups grapes

Combine neufchâtel cheese, juice and peel, mixing until well blended. Beat whipping cream until soft peaks form; gradually add sugar, beating until stiff peaks form. Fold into neufchâtel cheese mixture; chill. Layer fruit in $2^1/2$-quart glass serving bowl. Top with neufchâtel cheese mixture. Sprinkle with nuts, if desired. Chill.

8 servings

VARIATION
■ Substitute PHILADELPHIA BRAND Cream Cheese for Neufchâtel Cheese.

FLANK STEAK BEARNAISE

1   8-oz. pkg. PHILADELPHIA
    BRAND Cream Cheese,
    cubed
¼   cup milk
1   tablespoon green onion
    slices
½   teaspoon dried tarragon
    leaves, crushed
2   egg yolks, beaten
2   tablespoons dry white wine
1   tablespoon lemon juice
1   1½-lb. beef flank steak

In saucepan, combine cream cheese, milk, green onions and tarragon; stir over low heat until cream cheese is melted. Stir small amount of hot cream cheese mixture into egg yolks; return to hot mixture. Stir in wine and juice. Cook, stirring constantly, over low heat 1 minute or until thickened. Score steak on both sides. Place on rack of broiler pan. Broil on both sides to desired doneness. With knife slanted, carve steak across grain into thin slices. Serve with cream cheese mixture.

6 servings

SPARKLING CHERRY MOLD

1   17-oz. can pitted dark sweet
    cherries, undrained
1   3-oz. pkg. cherry flavored
    gelatin
1   cup boiling water
1   cup ginger ale
        *   *   *
1   3-oz. pkg. cherry flavored
    gelatin
1   cup boiling water
1   8-oz. pkg. PHILADELPHIA
    BRAND Cream Cheese,
    softened
    Lettuce

Drain cherries, reserving ¾ cup liquid. Dissolve gelatin in water; add ginger ale. Chill until thickened but not set; fold in cherries. Pour into lightly oiled 1½-quart mold; chill until almost set.

Dissolve gelatin in water; add reserved liquid. Gradually add gelatin mixture to cream cheese, mixing at medium speed on electric mixer until well blended. Pour over molded layer; chill until firm. Unmold onto lettuce-lined serving plate.

6 to 8 servings

SAVORY SUNDAY EGGS

¼   lb. bulk pork sausage
½   cup chopped onion
8   eggs, beaten
½   cup milk
    Dash of pepper
1   8-oz. pkg. PHILADELPHIA
    BRAND Cream Cheese,
    cubed
    Chopped chives

Brown sausage in large skillet; drain. Add onions; cook until tender. Add combined eggs, milk and pepper. Cook slowly, stirring occasionally, until eggs begin to set. Add cream cheese; continue cooking, stirring occasionally, until cream cheese is melted and eggs are set. Sprinkle with chives.

6 servings

STROGANOFF SUPERB

1 lb. beef sirloin steak, cut
    into thin strips
3 tablespoons PARKAY
    Margarine
1/2 cup chopped onion
1 4-oz. can mushrooms,
    drained
1/2 teaspoon salt
1/4 teaspoon dry mustard
1/4 teaspoon pepper
1 8-oz. pkg. PHILADELPHIA
    BRAND Cream Cheese,
    cubed
3/4 cup milk
    Hot parslied noodles

Brown steak in margarine in large skillet. Add onions, mushrooms and seasonings; cook until vegetables are tender. Add cream cheese and milk; stir over low heat until cream cheese is melted. Serve over noodles.

4 to 6 servings

MEXICAN FIESTA PIE

1/2 lb. ground beef
1/4 cup chopped onion
2 teaspoons chili powder
1 8-oz. pkg. PHILADELPHIA
    BRAND Cream Cheese,
    cubed
1 4-oz. can chopped green
    chilies, drained
1/2 cup pitted ripe olive slices
2 eggs, beaten
    *   *   *
3/4 cup flour
1/3 cup milk
2 eggs, beaten
1 tablespoon cornmeal
1 cup chopped tomato
1 cup (4 ozs.) shredded 100%
    Natural KRAFT Mild
    Cheddar Cheese

Brown meat; drain. Add onions; cook until tender. Stir in chili powder. Add cream cheese, chilies, olives and eggs; mix well.

Combine flour, milk and eggs; beat until smooth. Pour into greased 10-inch pie plate or quiche dish; sprinkle with cornmeal. Spoon meat mixture over batter to within 1/2 inch of outer edge of pan. Bake at 400°, 35 to 40 minutes or until golden brown. Top with tomatoes and cheddar cheese; continue baking 5 minutes.

6 to 8 servings

CREAMY LASAGNE

1 lb. ground beef
½ cup chopped onion
1 14½-oz. can tomatoes, cut up
1 6-oz. can tomato paste
⅓ cup water
1 garlic clove, minced
1 teaspoon dried oregano leaves, crushed
½ teaspoon salt
¼ teaspoon pepper
1 8-oz. pkg. PHILADELPHIA BRAND Cream Cheese, cubed
¼ cup milk
8 ozs. lasagne noodles, cooked, drained
2 6-oz. pkgs. 100% Natural KRAFT Low Moisture Part-Skim Mozzarella Cheese Slices
½ cup (2 ozs.) KRAFT Grated Parmesan Cheese

Brown meat in large skillet; drain. Add onions; cook until tender. Stir in tomatoes, tomato paste, water, garlic and seasonings. Cover; simmer 30 minutes. Combine cream cheese and milk in saucepan; stir over low heat until smooth. In 13 × 9-inch baking pan, layer half of noodles, meat mixture, cream cheese mixture, mozzarella and parmesan cheese; repeat layers. Bake at 350°, 30 minutes. Let stand 10 minutes before serving.

6 to 8 servings

MICROWAVE
Crumble meat into 1½-quart casserole. Microwave on High 4 to 5 minutes or until meat loses pink color when stirred; drain. Add onions, tomatoes, tomato paste, water and seasonings. Cover; microwave 12 minutes, stirring every 3 minutes. Microwave cream cheese and milk in 1-quart measure 3 to 4 minutes or until sauce is hot and smooth, stirring after 1½ minutes. In 13 × 9-inch baking dish, layer half of noodles, meat mixture, cream cheese mixture, mozzarella and parmesan cheese; repeat with remaining noodles, meat mixture and cream cheese mixture. Microwave 12 minutes, turning dish every 4 minutes. Top with remaining mozzarella and parmesan cheese. Microwave 4 to 6 minutes or until thoroughly heated. Let stand 10 minutes before serving.

DESSERT DISCOVERIES

STRAWBERRY TART GLACE

Pastry for 1-crust 9-inch pie

*   *   *

2 8-oz. pkgs. *Light*
 PHILADELPHIA BRAND
 Neufchâtel Cheese,
 softened
1/2 cup sugar
1 tablespoon milk
1/4 teaspoon vanilla
1 qt. strawberries, hulled
1 tablespoon cornstarch
1/4 cup water
 Few drops red food coloring
 (optional)

On lightly floured surface, roll pastry to 12-inch circle. Place in 10-inch quiche dish. Prick bottom and sides of pastry with fork. Bake at 450°, 9 to 11 minutes or until golden brown.

Combine neufchâtel cheese, 1/4 cup sugar, milk and vanilla, mixing at medium speed on electric mixer until well blended. Spread onto bottom of crust. Puree 1 cup strawberries. Top neufchâtel cheese mixture with remaining strawberries. Combine remaining sugar and cornstarch in saucepan; gradually add pureed strawberries and water. Cook, stirring constantly, over medium heat until mixture is clear and thickened. Stir in food coloring. Pour over strawberries; chill.

8 servings

VARIATIONS
■ Substitute 9-inch pie plate for 10-inch quiche dish.
■ Substitute almond extract for vanilla.
■ Substitute PHILADELPHIA BRAND Cream Cheese for Neufchâtel Cheese.

Strawberry Tart Glace

Favorite Layer Bars

FAVORITE LAYER BARS

1¹/₂ cups graham cracker crumbs
¹/₄ cup sugar
¹/₄ cup PARKAY Margarine,
   melted

* * *

1 8-oz. pkg. PHILADELPHIA
   BRAND Cream Cheese,
   softened
¹/₂ cup sugar
1 egg
³/₄ cup flaked coconut
³/₄ cup chopped nuts
1 6-oz. pkg. semi-sweet
   chocolate pieces

Combine crumbs, sugar and margarine; press onto bottom of 13 × 9-inch baking pan. Bake at 325°, 10 minutes.

Combine cream cheese, sugar and egg, mixing until well blended. Spread over crust. Sprinkle with combined coconut, nuts and chocolate; press lightly into surface. Bake at 350°, 25 to 30 minutes or until lightly browned. Cool; cut into bars.

Approximately 3 dozen

COCONUT TORTE

1 8-oz. container Soft
    PHILADELPHIA BRAND
    Cream Cheese
1/4 cup sugar
1 tablespoon orange juice
1/2 cup flaked coconut, toasted
1/4 cup sliced almonds, toasted
1 10 3/4-oz. frozen pound cake,
    thawed

Combine cream cheese, sugar and juice,
mixing until well blended. Add coconut
and almonds; mix well. Split cake into
three layers. Spread layers with frosting;
stack. Chill.

6 servings

CHILLY STRAWBERRY SOUFFLES

1 10-oz. pkg. frozen
    strawberries, thawed
2 envelopes unflavored gelatin
2 1/4 cups cold water
1 8-oz. pkg. *Light*
    PHILADELPHIA BRAND
    Neufchâtel Cheese,
    softened
1/4 cup sugar
1 tablespoon lemon juice
    Few drops red food coloring
    (optional)
2 cups thawed frozen whipped
    topping

Drain strawberries, reserving liquid.
Chop strawberries. Soften gelatin in 1/2
cup water; stir over low heat until
dissolved. Add remaining water.
Combine neufchâtel cheese and sugar,
mixing until well blended. Gradually
add gelatin mixture to neufchâtel
cheese mixture, mixing until well
blended. Stir in reserved liquid, juice
and food coloring. Chill, stirring
occasionally, until thickened but not set.
Beat with electric mixer or wire whisk
until smooth. Fold in strawberries and
whipped topping. Wrap 3-inch collar of
foil around individual dessert dishes or
cups; secure with tape. Pour mixture
into dishes; chill until firm. Remove
collar before serving.

8 to 10 servings

VARIATIONS
■ Substitute 1-quart souffle dish for
individual dessert dishes.
■ Substitute PHILADELPHIA BRAND
Cream Cheese for Neufchâtel Cheese.
Increase sugar to 2/3 cup. Substitute 1
cup whipping cream, whipped, for
whipped topping.

"PHILLY" CHOCOLATE SAUCE

1 8-oz. pkg. PHILADELPHIA
    BRAND Cream Cheese,
    cubed
1/3 cup milk
2 1-oz. squares unsweetened
    chocolate
2 cups sifted powdered sugar
1 teaspoon vanilla

Combine cream cheese, milk and chocolate; stir over low heat until smooth. Blend in remaining ingredients. Serve over poached pears, ice cream or cake.

2 cups

NOTE
This sauce can be refrigerated and then reheated.

EASY CHEESE DANISH

1 5-oz. can refrigerated
    buttermilk flaky biscuits
Soft PHILADELPHIA
    BRAND Cream Cheese
    with Strawberries or
    Pineapple
Flaked coconut

Separate dough into five biscuits. Make wide indentation in center of each biscuit; fill with approximately 1 tablespoonful cream cheese. Sprinkle with coconut. Bake at 375°, 12 to 15 minutes or until golden brown. Serve warm.

5 servings

VARIATION
■ Substitute Soft PHILADELPHIA BRAND Cream Cheese for Cream Cheese with Strawberries. Omit coconut. Sprinkle with cinnamon-sugar after baking.

"Philly" Chocolate Sauce

"Philly" Frosted Cookies

"PHILLY" FROSTED COOKIES

Oatmeal cookies or
  chocolate chip cookies
Soft PHILADELPHIA
  BRAND Cream Cheese
Peeled kiwi slices
Mandarin orange segments
Strawberry slices

For each serving, spread cookie with cream cheese; top with remaining ingredients as desired.

VARIATION
■ Substitute Soft PHILADELPHIA BRAND Cream Cheese with Strawberries for Soft Cream Cheese.

"PHILLY" BANANA PUDDING

12 vanilla wafers
 1 8-oz. container Soft
    PHILADELPHIA BRAND
    Cream Cheese
 2 tablespoons milk
 2 tablespoons sugar
 1 teaspoon vanilla
 2 cups thawed frozen whipped
    topping
 2 medium bananas, sliced

Line bottom and sides of 1-quart serving bowl with wafers. Combine cream cheese, milk, sugar and vanilla, mixing until well blended. Fold in remaining ingredients. Spoon into bowl; chill.

6 servings

MARBLE SQUARES

½ cup PARKAY Margarine
¾ cup water
1½ 1-oz. squares unsweetened
    chocolate
2 cups flour
2 cups sugar
1 teaspoon baking soda
½ teaspoon salt
2 eggs, beaten
½ cup sour cream

    *   *   *

1 8-oz. pkg. PHILADELPHIA
    BRAND Cream Cheese,
    softened
⅓ cup sugar
1 egg
1 6-oz. pkg. semi-sweet
    chocolate pieces

Combine margarine, water and chocolate in saucepan; bring to boil. Remove from heat. Stir in combined flour, sugar, baking soda and salt. Add eggs and sour cream; mix well. Pour into greased and floured 15 × 10 × 1-inch jelly roll pan.

Combine cream cheese and sugar, mixing until well blended. Blend in egg. Spoon over chocolate batter. Cut through batter with knife several times for marble effect. Sprinkle with chocolate pieces. Bake at 375°, 25 to 30 minutes or until wooden pick inserted in center comes out clean.

Approximately 2 dozen

Marble Squares

CREME DE MENTHE PIE

2 cups (24) crushed chocolate
  creme-filled cookies
1/4 cup PARKAY Margarine,
  melted

* * *

2 8-oz. pkgs. PHILADELPHIA
  BRAND Cream Cheese,
  softened
1 1/2 cups sifted powdered sugar
2 tablespoons green creme de
  menthe
2 cups whipping cream,
  whipped

Combine crumbs and margarine; press
onto bottom and sides of 9-inch pie
plate.

Combine cream cheese, sugar and
creme de menthe, mixing until well
blended. Fold in whipped cream; pour
into crust. Chill several hours or
overnight. Garnish with chocolate curls,
if desired.

8 servings

PINEAPPLE "PHILLY" PIE

Pastry for 1-crust 9-inch pie
1/3 cup sugar
1 tablespoon cornstarch
1 8 1/4-oz. can crushed
  pineapple, undrained

* * *

1 8-oz. pkg. PHILADELPHIA
  BRAND Cream Cheese,
  softened
1/2 cup sugar
1/2 teaspoon salt
2 eggs
1/2 cup milk
1/2 teaspoon vanilla
1/4 cup chopped pecans

On lightly floured surface, roll pastry to
12-inch circle. Place in 9-inch pie plate.
Turn under edge; flute. Combine sugar
and cornstarch in saucepan; stir in
pineapple. Cook, stirring constantly,
until mixture is clear and thickened.
Cool; spread onto bottom of pastry
shell.

Combine cream cheese, sugar and salt,
mixing until well blended. Add eggs,
one at a time, mixing well after each
addition. Blend in milk and vanilla. Pour
over pineapple mixture; sprinkle with
pecans. Bake at 350°, 35 minutes. Cool.
Garnish with pineapple slices, cut in
half, and maraschino cherry halves, if
desired.

8 servings

Top: Creme de Menthe Pie
Middle: Pineapple "Philly" Pie
Bottom: Paradise Pumpkin Pie (see page 54)

PARADISE PUMPKIN PIE

Pastry for 1-crust 9-inch pie
1 8-oz. pkg. PHILADELPHIA
   BRAND Cream Cheese,
   softened
¼ cup sugar
½ teaspoon vanilla
1 egg

On lightly floured surface, roll pastry to 12-inch circle. Place in 9-inch pie plate. Turn under edge; flute. Combine cream cheese, sugar and vanilla, mixing at medium speed on electric mixer until well blended. Blend in egg. Spread onto bottom of pastry shell.

* * *
1¼ cups canned pumpkin
1 cup evaporated milk
½ cup sugar
2 eggs, beaten
1 teaspoon cinnamon
¼ teaspoon ground ginger
¼ teaspoon ground nutmeg
   Dash of salt
   Maple syrup
   Pecan halves

Combine all remaining ingredients except syrup and pecans; mix well. Carefully pour over cream cheese mixture. Bake at 350°, 65 minutes. Cool. Brush with syrup; top with pecans.

8 servings

CINNAMON STREUSEL COFFEECAKE

½ cup chopped nuts
⅓ cup packed brown sugar
¼ cup flour
½ teaspoon cinnamon
¼ cup PARKAY Margarine

* * *
1 8-oz. pkg. PHILADELPHIA
   BRAND Cream Cheese,
   softened
1 cup granulated sugar
½ cup PARKAY Margarine
2 eggs
1 teaspoon vanilla
1¾ cups flour
1 teaspoon baking powder
½ teaspoon baking soda
¼ teaspoon salt
¼ cup milk

Combine nuts, brown sugar, flour and cinnamon; cut in margarine until mixture resembles coarse crumbs.

Combine cream cheese, granulated sugar and margarine, mixing at medium speed on electric mixer until well blended. Blend in eggs and vanilla. Add combined dry ingredients alternately with milk, mixing well after each addition. Pour batter into greased and floured 13×9-inch baking pan. Sprinkle with nut mixture. Bake at 350°, 30 minutes or until wooden pick inserted in center comes out clean.

12 servings

APRICOT CRUMBLE CAKE

1 8-oz. pkg. PHILADELPHIA
   BRAND Cream Cheese,
   softened
1/2 cup PARKAY Margarine
1 1/4 cups granulated sugar
1/4 cup milk
2 eggs
1 teaspoon vanilla
1 3/4 cups flour
1 teaspoon baking powder
1/2 teaspoon baking soda
1/4 teaspoon salt
1 10-oz. jar KRAFT Apricot or
   Peach Preserves

     *   *   *

2 cups flaked coconut
2/3 cup packed brown sugar
1 teaspoon cinnamon
1/3 cup PARKAY Margarine,
   melted

Combine cream cheese, margarine and granulated sugar, mixing at medium speed on electric mixer until well blended. Gradually add milk, mixing well after each addition. Blend in eggs and vanilla. Add combined dry ingredients to cream cheese mixture; mix well. Pour half of batter into greased and floured 13 × 9-inch baking pan. Dot with preserves; cover with remaining batter. Bake at 350°, 35 to 40 minutes or until wooden pick inserted in center comes out clean.

Combine coconut, brown sugar, cinnamon and margarine; mix well. Spread onto cake; broil 5 minutes, or until golden brown.

16 servings

Apricot Crumble Cake

CHERRY NUT CAKE

1 8-oz. pkg. PHILADELPHIA
   BRAND Cream Cheese,
   softened
1 cup PARKAY Margarine
1½ cups granulated sugar
1½ teaspoons vanilla
4 eggs
2¼ cups sifted cake flour
1½ teaspoons baking powder
¾ cup chopped maraschino
   cherries, well-drained
½ cup chopped pecans
     *   *   *
½ cup finely chopped pecans
1½ cups sifted powdered sugar
2 tablespoons milk

Combine cream cheese, margarine, granulated sugar and vanilla, mixing at medium speed on electric mixer until well blended. Add eggs, one at a time, mixing well after each addition. Sift together 2 cups flour and baking powder. Gradually add to cream cheese mixture; mix well. Toss remaining flour with cherries and pecans; fold into batter.

Grease 10-inch tube or fluted tube pan; sprinkle with finely chopped pecans. Pour batter into pan. Bake at 325°, 1 hour and 10 minutes. Cool 5 minutes; remove from pan. Cool. Glaze with combined powdered sugar and milk. Garnish with additional pecan halves and maraschino cherry halves, if desired.

10 to 12 servings

VARIATIONS

■ Omit finely chopped nuts. Pour batter into three greased and floured 1-lb. coffee cans. Bake at 325°, 1 hour.

■ Omit finely chopped nuts. Pour batter into four greased and floured 1-lb. shortening cans. Bake at 325°, 1 hour.

■ Omit finely chopped nuts. Pour batter into five greased and floured 5¾ × 3¼-inch loaf pans. Bake at 325°, 45 to 50 minutes.

■ Substitute greased 9-inch springform pan with ring insert for 10-inch tube or fluted tube pan.

■ Substitute ¾ cup chopped dried apricots for maraschino cherries and 2 tablespoons orange juice and 1 teaspoon grated orange peel for milk.

■ Substitute 2 cups all-purpose flour for sifted cake flour.

MAKE AHEAD

Bake cake; wrap securely in moisture-vaporproof wrap. Freeze. When ready to serve, thaw, wrapped, at room temperature for 24 hours.

Cherry Nut Cake

PECAN TASSIES

1 8-oz. pkg. PHILADELPHIA
    BRAND Cream Cheese,
    softened
1 cup PARKAY Margarine
2 cups flour
2 eggs, beaten
1½ cups packed brown sugar
2 teaspoons vanilla
1½ cups chopped pecans

Combine cream cheese and margarine, mixing until well blended. Add flour; mix well. Chill. Divide dough into quarters; divide each quarter into 12 balls. Press each ball onto bottom and sides of miniature muffin pans. Combine eggs, brown sugar and vanilla; stir in pecans. Spoon into pastry shells, filling each cup. Bake at 325°, 30 minutes or until pastry is golden brown. Cool 5 minutes; remove from pans. Sprinkle with powdered sugar, if desired.

4 dozen

CHOCOLATE "PHILLY" FUDGE

4 cups sifted powdered sugar
1 8-oz. pkg. PHILADELPHIA
    BRAND Cream Cheese,
    softened
4 1-oz. squares unsweetened
    chocolate, melted
1 teaspoon vanilla
    Dash of salt
½ cup chopped nuts

Gradually add sugar to cream cheese, mixing well after each addition. Add remaining ingredients; mix well. Spread into greased 8-inch square pan. Chill several hours; cut into squares.

1¾ pounds

VARIATIONS

■ Omit vanilla and nuts; add few drops peppermint extract and ¼ cup crushed peppermint candy. Sprinkle with additional ¼ cup crushed peppermint candy before chilling.

■ Omit nuts; add 1 cup shredded coconut. Garnish with additional coconut.

■ Omit nuts; add ½ cup chopped maraschino cherries, drained. Garnish with whole cherries.

Top: Pecan Tassies
Middle: Chocolate "Philly" Fudge
Bottom: "Philly" Apricot Cookies (see page 60)

"PHILLY" APRICOT COOKIES

1½ cups PARKAY Margarine
1½ cups granulated sugar
 1 8-oz. pkg. PHILADELPHIA
   BRAND Cream Cheese,
   softened
 2 eggs
 2 tablespoons lemon juice
1½ teaspoons grated lemon peel
4½ cups flour
1½ teaspoons baking powder
   KRAFT Apricot Preserves
   Powdered sugar

Combine margarine, granulated sugar and cream cheese, mixing until well blended. Blend in eggs, juice and peel. Add combined flour and baking powder; mix well. Chill several hours. Shape level measuring tablespoonfuls of dough into balls. Place on ungreased cookie sheet; flatten slightly. Indent centers; fill with preserves. Bake at 350°, 15 minutes. Cool; sprinkle with powdered sugar.

Approximately 7 dozen

FRUIT PIZZA

 1 20-oz. pkg. PILLSBURY'S
   BEST Refrigerated Sugar
   Cookies
        *   *   *
 1 8-oz. pkg. PHILADELPHIA
   BRAND Cream Cheese,
   softened
⅓ cup sugar
½ teaspoon vanilla
   Assorted fruit
½ cup KRAFT Orange
   Marmalade, Peach or
   Apricot Preserves
 2 tablespoons water

Freeze cookie dough 1 hour. Slice into ⅛-inch slices. Line foil-lined 14-inch pizza pan with slices, overlapping edges slightly. Bake at 375°, 12 minutes or until golden brown. Cool. Invert onto serving plate; carefully remove foil. Turn right side up.

Combine cream cheese, sugar and vanilla, mixing until well blended. Spread over crust. Arrange fruit over cream cheese layer. Glaze with combined marmalade and water; chill. Cut into wedges.

10 to 12 servings

VARIATION
■Substitute Soft PHILADELPHIA BRAND Cream Cheese for Regular Cream Cheese.

Fruit Pizza

PUMPKIN CHEESE BREAD

2½ cups sugar
1 8-oz. pkg. PHILADELPHIA BRAND Cream Cheese, softened
½ cup PARKAY Margarine
4 eggs
1 16-oz. can pumpkin
3½ cups flour
2 teaspoons baking soda
1 teaspoon salt
1 teaspoon cinnamon
½ teaspoon baking powder
¼ teaspoon ground cloves
1 cup chopped nuts

Combine sugar, cream cheese and margarine, mixing at medium speed on electric mixer until well blended. Add eggs, one at a time, mixing well after each addition. Blend in pumpkin. Add combined dry ingredients, mixing just until moistened. Fold in nuts. Pour into two greased and floured 9 x 5-inch loaf pans. Bake at 350°, 1 hour or until wooden pick inserted in center comes out clean. Cool 5 minutes; remove from pans.

2 loaves

FROSTY ORANGE DESSERT

1 3-oz. pkg. orange flavored gelatin
1 cup boiling water
½ cup cold water
⅓ cup orange juice
1 teaspoon grated orange peel
1 8-oz. pkg. *Light* PHILADELPHIA BRAND Neufchâtel Cheese, softened
¼ cup sugar

Dissolve gelatin in boiling water; add cold water, juice and peel. Combine neufchâtel cheese and sugar, mixing until well blended. Gradually add gelatin mixture to neufchâtel cheese mixture, mixing until blended. Chill, stirring occasionally, until thickened but not set. Beat with electric mixer until fluffy. Spoon into individual parfait glasses; chill several hours or overnight.

6 to 8 servings

VARIATIONS
■ Substitute PHILADELPHIA BRAND Cream Cheese for Neufchâtel Cheese.
■ Substitute lime flavored gelatin for orange flavored gelatin. Reduce orange juice to ¼ cup. Add 2 tablespoons lime juice with orange juice. Substitute lime peel for orange peel.

Pumpkin Cheese Bread

BAVARIAN LEMON CREME

1 envelope unflavored gelatin
½ cup cold water
2 8-oz. pkgs. *Light*
   PHILADELPHIA BRAND
   Neufchâtel Cheese,
   softened
⅓ cup sugar
¼ cup milk
¼ cup lemon juice
½ teaspoon grated lemon peel
2 egg whites
2 cups thawed frozen whipped
   topping
   Lemon Sauce

Soften gelatin in water; stir over low heat until dissolved. Combine neufchâtel cheese and sugar, mixing until well blended. Gradually add gelatin, milk, juice and peel, mixing until blended. Chill, stirring occasionally, until thickened but not set. Beat with electric mixer or wire whisk until smooth. Beat egg whites until stiff peaks form. Fold egg whites and whipped topping into neufchâtel cheese mixture. Pour into lightly oiled 1½-quart mold; chill until firm. Unmold; serve with Lemon Sauce.

8 to 10 servings

VARIATION
■ Substitute PHILADELPHIA BRAND Cream Cheese for Neufchâtel Cheese. Increase sugar to ½ cup. Substitute 1 cup whipping cream, whipped, for whipped topping.

LEMON SAUCE

¾ cup sugar
2 tablespoons cornstarch
¼ cup water
¼ cup lemon juice
2 egg yolks, beaten

Combine sugar and cornstarch in saucepan; gradually add water and juice. Cook, stirring constantly, until mixture is clear and thickened. Stir small amount of hot mixture into egg yolks; return to hot mixture. Cook, stirring constantly, over low heat until thickened. Cool.

CHOCOLATEY PEANUT TREATS

1 8-oz. container Soft
   PHILADELPHIA BRAND
   Cream Cheese
½ cup peanut butter
1 6-oz. pkg. semi-sweet
   chocolate pieces, melted
2¼ cups graham cracker crumbs
⅔ cup finely chopped peanuts

Combine cream cheese and peanut butter, mixing until well blended. Blend in chocolate. Stir in graham cracker crumbs; mix well. Shape into 1-inch balls. Roll in peanuts; chill.

4 dozen

VARIATION
■ Omit peanuts. Prepare, shape and chill dough as directed. Roll in powdered sugar just before serving.

"Philly" Fruit Clouds

"PHILLY" FRUIT CLOUDS

1 8-oz. pkg. PHILADELPHIA
   BRAND Cream Cheese,
   softened
½ cup sugar
1 tablespoon lemon juice
2 teaspoons grated lemon peel
1 cup whipping cream,
   whipped
   Assorted fruit

Combine cream cheese, sugar, juice and peel, mixing until well blended. Fold in whipped cream. With back of spoon, shape on wax paper-lined cookie sheet to form ten shells; freeze. Fill each shell with fruit. Garnish with fresh mint, if desired.

10 servings

VARIATIONS

■ Prepare cream cheese mixture as directed. Spread into 8-inch square pan; freeze. Cut into squares; top with fruit.
■ Substitute *Light* PHILADELPHIA BRAND Neufchâtel Cheese for Cream Cheese.

Peach Surprise Pie

PEACH SURPRISE PIE

2 8-oz. pkgs. *Light*
   PHILADELPHIA BRAND
   Neufchâtel Cheese,
   softened
¼ cup sugar
½ teaspoon vanilla
   Pastry for 1-crust 9-inch pie,
   baked
1 16-oz. can peach slices,
   drained
¼ cup KRAFT Red Raspberry
   Preserves
1 teaspoon lemon juice

Combine neufchâtel cheese, sugar and vanilla, mixing until well blended. Spread onto bottom of crust; chill several hours or overnight. Top with peaches just before serving. Combine preserves and juice, mixing until well blended. Spoon over peaches. Garnish with fresh mint, if desired.

6 to 8 servings

DELIGHTFUL DESSERT PANCAKE

1 8-oz. pkg. *Light*
  PHILADELPHIA BRAND
  Neufchâtel Cheese,
  softened
3 tablespoons honey
1 teaspoon grated lemon peel
1 teaspoon lemon juice
      *   *   *
¹/₂ cup milk
¹/₂ cup flour
¹/₄ teaspoon salt
2 eggs, beaten
1 tablespoon PARKAY
  Margarine
2 cups assorted fruit
¹/₄ cup toasted flaked coconut

Combine neufchâtel cheese, honey, peel and juice, mixing until well blended. Chill.

Gradually add milk to combined flour and salt; beat until smooth. Beat in eggs. Heat heavy 10-inch ovenproof skillet in 450° oven until very hot. Add margarine to coat skillet; pour in batter immediately. Bake on lowest oven rack at 450°, 10 minutes. Reduce oven temperature to 350°; continue baking 10 minutes or until golden brown. Fill with fruit; sprinkle with coconut. Serve immediately with neufchâtel cheese mixture.

6 to 8 servings

TORTONI SQUARES

1 envelope unflavored gelatin
¹/₂ cup cold water
2 8-oz. containers Soft
  PHILADELPHIA BRAND
  Cream Cheese
2 tablespoons sugar
1 17-oz. can apricot halves,
  drained, chopped
2 tablespoons chopped
  almonds, toasted
¹/₄ teaspoon rum flavoring
2 cups thawed frozen whipped
  topping
2 cups macaroon cookies,
  crumbled

Soften gelatin in water; stir over low heat until dissolved. Cool. Combine cream cheese and sugar, mixing until well blended. Gradually add gelatin, mixing until blended. Stir in apricots, almonds and flavoring. Fold in whipped topping. Place macaroons on bottom of 9-inch square baking pan; top with cream cheese mixture. Chill; cut into squares.

9 servings

CHEESECAKE CLASSICS

MINIATURE CHEESECAKES

⅓ cup graham cracker crumbs
1 tablespoon PARKAY
    Margarine, melted
1 tablespoon sugar
    *   *   *
1 8-oz. pkg. PHILADELPHIA
    BRAND Cream Cheese,
    softened
¼ cup sugar
1½ teaspoons lemon juice
½ teaspoon grated lemon peel
¼ teaspoon vanilla
1 egg
    KRAFT Strawberry or
    Apricot Preserves

Combine crumbs, margarine and sugar. Press rounded measuring tablespoonful of crumb mixture onto bottom of each of six paper-lined muffin cups. Bake at 325°, 5 minutes.

Combine cream cheese, sugar, juice, peel and vanilla, mixing at medium speed on electric mixer until well blended. Blend in egg; pour over crust, filling each cup ¾ full. Bake at 325°, 25 minutes. Cool before removing from pan. Chill. Top with preserves just before serving.

6 servings

VARIATION
■ Substitute fresh fruit for KRAFT Preserves.

MAKE AHEAD
Wrap chilled cheesecakes individually in moisture-vaporproof wrap; freeze. Let stand at room temperature 40 minutes before serving.

Miniature Cheesecakes

BLACK FOREST CHEESECAKE DELIGHT

1 cup chocolate wafer crumbs
3 tablespoons PARKAY
  Margarine, melted
        *   *   *
2 8-oz. pkgs. PHILADELPHIA
  BRAND Cream Cheese,
  softened
²/₃ cup sugar
2 eggs
1 6-oz. pkg. semi-sweet
  chocolate pieces, melted
¼ teaspoon almond extract
        *   *   *
1 21-oz. can cherry pie filling
  Frozen whipped topping,
  thawed

Combine crumbs and margarine; press onto bottom of 9-inch springform pan. Bake at 350°, 10 minutes.

Combine cream cheese and sugar, mixing at medium speed on electric mixer until well blended. Add eggs, one at a time, mixing well after each addition. Blend in chocolate and extract; pour over crust. Bake at 350°, 45 minutes. Loosen cake from rim of pan; cool before removing rim of pan. Chill.

Top cheesecake with pie filling and whipped topping just before serving.

10 to 12 servings

COCONUT CHOCO CHEESECAKE

1 cup graham cracker crumbs
3 tablespoons sugar
3 tablespoons PARKAY
  Margarine, melted
        *   *   *
2 1-oz. squares unsweetened
  chocolate
2 tablespoons PARKAY
  Margarine
2 8-oz. pkgs. PHILADELPHIA
  BRAND Cream Cheese,
  softened
1¼ cups sugar
¼ teaspoon salt
5 eggs
1¹/₃ cups (3.5 oz. can) flaked
  coconut
        *   *   *
1 cup sour cream
2 tablespoons sugar
2 tablespoons brandy

Combine crumbs, sugar and margarine. Press onto bottom of 9-inch springform pan. Bake at 350°, 10 minutes.

Melt chocolate and margarine over low heat, stirring until smooth. Cool. Combine cream cheese, sugar and salt, mixing at medium speed on electric mixer until well blended. Add eggs, one at a time, mixing well after each addition. Blend in chocolate mixture and coconut; pour over crust. Bake at 350°, 55 to 60 minutes or until set.

Combine sour cream, sugar and brandy; spread over cheesecake. Bake at 300°, 5 minutes. Loosen cake from rim of pan; cool before removing rim of pan. Chill.

10 to 12 servings

Black Forest Cheesecake Delight

CHERRY CHEESECAKE

1 cup graham cracker crumbs
3 tablespoons sugar
3 tablespoons PARKAY
  Margarine, melted
    *   *   *
3 8-oz. pkgs. PHILADELPHIA
  BRAND Cream Cheese,
  softened
3/4 cup sugar
3 eggs
1 teaspoon vanilla
1 21-oz. can cherry pie filling

Combine crumbs, sugar and margarine; press onto bottom of 9-inch springform pan. Bake at 325°, 10 minutes.

Combine cream cheese and sugar, mixing at medium speed on electric mixer until well blended. Add eggs, one at a time, mixing well after each addition. Blend in vanilla; pour over crust. Bake at 450°, 10 minutes. Reduce oven temperature to 250°; continue baking 25 to 30 minutes or until set. Loosen cake from rim of pan; cool before removing rim of pan. Chill. Top with pie filling just before serving.

10 to 12 servings

SUN-SATIONAL CHEESECAKE

1 cup graham cracker crumbs
3 tablespoons sugar
3 tablespoons PARKAY
  Margarine, melted
    *   *   *
3 8-oz. pkgs. PHILADELPHIA
  BRAND Cream Cheese,
  softened
1 cup sugar
3 tablespoons flour
2 tablespoons lemon juice
1 tablespoon grated lemon
  peel
1/2 teaspoon vanilla
4 eggs (1 separated)
    *   *   *
3/4 cup sugar
2 tablespoons cornstarch
1/2 cup water
1/4 cup lemon juice

Combine crumbs, sugar and margarine; press onto bottom of 9-inch springform pan. Bake at 325°, 10 minutes.

Combine cream cheese, sugar, flour, juice, peel and vanilla, mixing at medium speed on electric mixer until well blended. Add three eggs, one at a time, mixing well after each addition. Beat in remaining egg white; reserve yolk for glaze. Pour over crust. Bake at 450°, 10 minutes. Reduce oven temperature to 250°; continue baking 30 minutes. Loosen cake from rim of pan; cool before removing rim of pan.

Combine sugar and cornstarch in saucepan; stir in water and juice. Cook, stirring constantly, until clear and thickened. Add small amount of hot mixture to slightly beaten egg yolk. Return to hot mixture; cook 3 minutes, stirring constantly. Cool slightly. Spoon over cheesecake; chill.

10 to 12 servings

Marble Cheesecake

MARBLE CHEESECAKE

1 cup graham cracker crumbs
3 tablespoons sugar
3 tablespoons PARKAY
    Margarine, melted
      *   *   *
3 8-oz. pkgs. PHILADELPHIA
    BRAND Cream Cheese,
    softened
3/4 cup sugar
1 teaspoon vanilla
3 eggs
1 1-oz. square unsweetened
    chocolate, melted

Combine crumbs, sugar and margarine; press onto bottom of 9-inch springform pan. Bake at 350°, 10 minutes.

Combine cream cheese, sugar and vanilla, mixing at medium speed on electric mixer until well blended. Add eggs, one at a time, mixing well after each addition. Blend chocolate into 1 cup batter. Spoon plain and chocolate batters alternately over crust; cut through batters with knife several times for marble effect. Bake at 450°, 10 minutes. Reduce oven temperature to 250°; continue baking 30 minutes. Loosen cake from rim of pan; cool before removing rim of pan. Chill.

10 to 12 servings

COCOA-NUT MERINGUE CHEESECAKE ▬▬▬▬▬

1 7-oz. pkg. flaked coconut, toasted
¼ cup chopped pecans
3 tablespoons PARKAY Margarine, melted
* * *
2 8-oz. pkgs. PHILADELPHIA BRAND Cream Cheese, softened
⅓ cup sugar
3 tablespoons cocoa
2 tablespoons water
1 teaspoon vanilla
3 eggs, separated
* * *
Dash of salt
1 7-oz. jar KRAFT Marshmallow Creme
½ cup chopped pecans

Combine coconut, pecans and margarine; press onto bottom of 9-inch springform pan.

Combine cream cheese, sugar, cocoa, water and vanilla, mixing at medium speed on electric mixer until well blended. Blend in egg yolks; pour over crust. Bake at 350°, 30 minutes. Loosen cake from rim of pan; cool before removing rim of pan.

Beat egg whites and salt until foamy; gradually add marshmallow creme, beating until stiff peaks form. Sprinkle pecans over cheesecake to within ½ inch of outer edge. Carefully spread marshmallow creme mixture over top of cheesecake to seal. Bake at 350°, 15 minutes. Cool.

10 to 12 servings

COOKIES AND CREAM CHEESECAKE ▬▬▬▬▬

2 cups (24) crushed creme-filled chocolate cookies
6 tablespoons PARKAY Margarine, softened
* * *
1 envelope unflavored gelatin
¼ cup cold water
1 8-oz. pkg. PHILADELPHIA BRAND Cream Cheese, softened
½ cup sugar
¾ cup milk
1 cup whipping cream, whipped
1¼ cups (10) coarsely chopped creme-filled chocolate cookies

Combine cookie crumbs and margarine; press onto bottom and sides of 9-inch springform pan.

Soften gelatin in water; stir over low heat until dissolved. Combine cream cheese and sugar, mixing at medium speed on electric mixer until well blended. Gradually add gelatin and milk, mixing until blended. Chill until mixture is thickened but not set. Fold in whipped cream. Reserve 1½ cups cream cheese mixture; pour remaining cream cheese mixture over crust. Top with cookies and reserved cream cheese mixture. Chill until firm.

8 servings

Cocoa-Nut Meringue Cheesecake

CHOCOLATE VELVET CHEESECAKE

1 cup vanilla wafer crumbs
1/2 cup chopped pecans
3 tablespoons granulated
   sugar
1/4 cup PARKAY Margarine,
   melted

     *   *   *

2 8-oz. pkgs. PHILADELPHIA
   BRAND Cream Cheese,
   softened
1/2 cup packed brown sugar
2 eggs
1 6-oz. pkg. semi-sweet
   chocolate pieces, melted
3 tablespoons almond flavored
   liqueur

     *   *   *

2 cups sour cream
2 tablespoons granulated
   sugar

Combine crumbs, pecans, granulated sugar and margarine; press onto bottom of 9-inch springform pan. Bake at 325°, 10 minutes.

Combine cream cheese and brown sugar, mixing at medium speed on electric mixer until well blended. Add eggs, one at a time, mixing well after each addition. Blend in chocolate and liqueur; pour over crust. Bake at 325°, 35 minutes.

Increase oven temperature to 425°. Combine sour cream and granulated sugar; carefully spread over cheesecake. Bake at 425°, 10 minutes. Loosen cake from rim of pan; cool before removing rim of pan. Chill.

10 to 12 servings

VARIATION
■ Substitute 2 tablespoons milk and 1/4 teaspoon almond extract for almond flavored liqueur.

VERY SMOOTH CHEESECAKE

1 cup graham cracker crumbs
3 tablespoons sugar
3 tablespoons PARKAY
   Margarine, melted

     *   *   *

1 envelope unflavored gelatin
1/4 cup cold water
1 8-oz. pkg. PHILADELPHIA
   BRAND Cream Cheese,
   softened
1/2 cup sugar
   Dash of salt
1 10-oz. pkg. frozen
   strawberries, thawed
   Milk
1 cup whipping cream,
   whipped

Combine crumbs, sugar and margarine; press onto bottom of 9-inch springform pan. Bake at 325°, 10 minutes. Cool.

Soften gelatin in water; stir over low heat until dissolved. Combine cream cheese, sugar and salt, mixing at medium speed on electric mixer until well blended. Drain strawberries, reserving liquid. Add enough milk to liquid to measure 1 cup. Gradually add combined milk mixture and gelatin to cream cheese, mixing until blended. Chill until slightly thickened. Fold in whipped cream and strawberries; pour over crust. Chill until firm.

10 to 12 servings

Northwest Cheesecake Supreme

NORTHWEST CHEESECAKE SUPREME

1 cup graham cracker crumbs
3 tablespoons sugar
3 tablespoons PARKAY
    Margarine, melted
        *   *   *
4 8-oz. pkgs. PHILADELPHIA
    BRAND Cream Cheese,
    softened
1 cup sugar
3 tablespoons flour
4 eggs
1 cup sour cream
1 tablespoon vanilla
1 21-oz. can cherry pie filling

Combine crumbs, sugar and margarine; press onto bottom of 9-inch springform pan. Bake at 325°, 10 minutes.

Combine cream cheese, sugar and flour, mixing at medium speed on electric mixer until well blended. Add eggs, one at a time, mixing well after each addition. Blend in sour cream and vanilla; pour over crust. Bake at 450°, 10 minutes. Reduce oven temperature to 250°; continue baking 1 hour. Loosen cake from rim of pan; cool before removing rim of pan. Chill. Top with pie filling just before serving.

10 to 12 servings

VARIATION
■ Substitute 1½ cups finely chopped nuts and 2 tablespoons sugar for graham cracker crumbs and sugar.

Rum Raisin Cheesecake

RUM RAISIN CHEESECAKE

1 cup old fashioned or quick-cooking oats, uncooked
¼ cup chopped nuts
3 tablespoons PARKAY Margarine, melted
3 tablespoons packed brown sugar

*   *   *

2 8-oz. pkgs. PHILADELPHIA BRAND Cream Cheese, softened
⅓ cup granulated sugar
¼ cup flour
2 eggs
½ cup sour cream
3 tablespoons rum
2 tablespoons PARKAY Margarine
⅓ cup packed brown sugar
⅓ cup raisins
¼ cup chopped nuts
2 tablespoons old fashioned or quick-cooking oats, uncooked

Combine oats, nuts, margarine and brown sugar; press onto bottom of 9-inch springform pan. Bake at 350°, 15 minutes.

Combine cream cheese, granulated sugar and 2 tablespoons flour, mixing at medium speed on electric mixer until well blended. Add eggs, one at a time, mixing well after each addition. Blend in sour cream and rum; mix well. Pour over crust. Cut margarine into combined remaining flour and brown sugar until mixture resembles coarse crumbs. Stir in raisins, nuts and oats. Sprinkle over cream cheese mixture. Bake at 350°, 50 minutes. Loosen cake from rim of pan; cool before removing rim of pan.

10 to 12 servings

HEAVENLY DESSERT CHEESECAKE

1 tablespoon graham cracker crumbs
1 cup low fat (1% to 2%) cottage cheese
2 8-oz. pkgs. *Light* PHILADELPHIA BRAND Neufchâtel Cheese, softened
2/3 cup sugar
2 tablespoons flour
3 eggs
2 tablespoons skim milk
1/4 teaspoon almond extract

Lightly grease bottom of 9-inch springform pan. Sprinkle with crumbs. Dust bottom; remove excess crumbs. Place cottage cheese in blender container. Cover; process on high speed until smooth. In large mixing bowl of electric mixer, combine cottage cheese, neufchâtel cheese, sugar and flour, mixing at medium speed until well blended. Add eggs, one at a time, mixing well after each addition. Blend in milk and extract; pour into pan. Bake at 325°, 45 to 50 minutes or until center is almost set. (Center of cheesecake appears soft but firms upon cooling.) Loosen cake from rim of pan; cool before removing rim of pan. Chill. Top with fresh strawberry slices or blueberries, if desired.

10 to 12 servings

VARIATION

■ Prepare pan as directed; omit blender method. Place cottage cheese in large bowl of electric mixer; beat cottage cheese at high speed until smooth. Add neufchâtel cheese, sugar and flour, mixing at medium speed until well blended. Continue as directed.

PEPPERMINT CHEESECAKE ━━━━━

1 cup chocolate wafer crumbs
3 tablespoons PARKAY
  Margarine, melted
      *   *   *
1 envelope unflavored gelatin
1/4 cup cold water
2 8-oz. containers Soft
  PHILADELPHIA BRAND
  Cream Cheese
1/2 cup sugar
1/2 cup milk
1/4 cup crushed peppermint
  candy
1 cup whipping cream,
  whipped
2 1.45-oz. milk chocolate
  candy bars, finely chopped

Combine crumbs and margarine; press onto bottom of 9-inch springform pan. Bake at 350°, 10 minutes. Cool.

Soften gelatin in water; stir over low heat until dissolved. Combine cream cheese and sugar, mixing at medium speed on electric mixer until well blended. Gradually add gelatin, milk and peppermint candy, mixing until blended; chill until thickened but not set. Fold in whipped cream and chocolate; pour over crust. Chill until firm. Garnish with additional whipping cream, whipped, combined with crushed peppermint candy, if desired.

10 to 12 servings

LIME DELICIOUS CHEESECAKE ━━━━━

1 1/4 cups zwieback toast crumbs
2 tablespoons sugar
1/3 cup PARKAY Margarine,
  melted
      *   *   *
1 envelope unflavored gelatin
1/4 cup cold water
1/4 cup lime juice
3 eggs, separated
1/2 cup sugar
1 1/2 teaspoons grated lime peel
2 8-oz. pkgs. *Light*
  PHILADELPHIA BRAND
  Neufchâtel Cheese,
  softened
  Few drops green food
  coloring (optional)
2 cups thawed frozen whipped
  topping

Combine crumbs, sugar and margarine; press onto bottom of 9-inch springform pan. Bake at 325°, 10 minutes. Cool.

Soften gelatin in water; stir over low heat until dissolved. Add juice, egg yolks, 1/4 cup sugar and peel; cook, stirring constantly, over medium heat 5 minutes. Cool. Gradually add gelatin mixture to neufchâtel cheese, mixing at medium speed on electric mixer until well blended. Stir in food coloring. Beat egg whites until foamy; gradually add remaining sugar, beating until stiff peaks form. Fold egg whites and whipped topping into neufchâtel cheese mixture; pour over crust. Chill until firm. Garnish with additional lime peel, if desired.

10 to 12 servings

Peppermint Cheesecake

CHOCOLATE TURTLE CHEESECAKE ▬▬

2 cups vanilla wafer crumbs
6 tablespoons PARKAY Margarine, melted

* * *

1 14-oz. bag KRAFT Caramels
1 5-oz. can evaporated milk
1 cup chopped pecans, toasted
2 8-oz. pkgs. PHILADELPHIA BRAND Cream Cheese, softened
1/2 cup sugar
1 teaspoon vanilla
2 eggs
1/2 cup semi-sweet chocolate pieces, melted

Combine crumbs and margarine; press onto bottom and sides of 9-inch springform pan. Bake at 350°, 10 minutes.

In 1 1/2-quart heavy saucepan, melt caramels with milk over low heat, stirring frequently, until smooth. Pour over crust. Top with pecans. Combine cream cheese, sugar and vanilla, mixing at medium speed on electric mixer until well blended. Add eggs, one at a time, mixing well after each addition. Blend in chocolate; pour over pecans. Bake at 350°, 40 minutes. Loosen cake from rim of pan; cool before removing rim of pan. Chill. Garnish with whipped cream, additional chopped nuts and maraschino cherries, if desired.

10 to 12 servings

Chocolate Turtle Cheesecake

PEANUT BUTTER AND JELLY CHEESECAKE

1 cup old fashioned or quick-
    cooking oats
1/4 cup chopped peanuts
3 tablespoons packed brown
    sugar
3 tablespoons PARKAY
    Margarine, melted
       *   *   *
2 8-oz. pkgs. PHILADELPHIA
    BRAND Cream Cheese,
    softened
1 cup granulated sugar
1/2 cup chunk style peanut
    butter
3 tablespoons flour
4 eggs
1/2 cup milk
1/2 cup KRAFT Grape Jelly

Combine oats, peanuts, brown sugar and margarine; press onto bottom of 9-inch springform pan. Bake at 325°, 10 minutes.

Combine cream cheese, granulated sugar, peanut butter and flour, mixing at medium speed on electric mixer until well blended. (Batter will be very stiff.) Add eggs, one at a time, mixing well after each addition. Blend in milk; pour over crust. Bake at 450°, 10 minutes. Reduce oven temperature to 250°; continue baking 40 minutes. Loosen cake from rim of pan; cool before removing rim of pan. Stir jelly until smooth; drizzle over cheesecake in criss-cross pattern to form lattice design. Chill.

10 to 12 servings

VARIATION
■ For crust: Substitute 1 cup graham cracker crumbs for oats and peanuts. Substitute granulated sugar for brown sugar.

ROCKY ROAD CHEESECAKE

1 cup chocolate wafer crumbs
3 tablespoons PARKAY
    Margarine, melted
       *   *   *
1 envelope unflavored gelatin
1/4 cup cold water
2 8-oz. containers Soft
    PHILADELPHIA BRAND
    Cream Cheese
3/4 cup sugar
1/3 cup cocoa
1/2 teaspoon vanilla
2 cups KRAFT Miniature
    Marshmallows
1 cup whipping cream,
    whipped
1/2 cup chopped nuts

Combine crumbs and margarine; press onto bottom of 9-inch springform pan. Bake at 350°, 10 minutes. Cool.

Soften gelatin in water; stir over low heat until dissolved. Combine cream cheese, sugar, cocoa and vanilla, mixing at medium speed on electric mixer until well blended. Gradually add gelatin, mixing until blended. Fold in remaining ingredients; pour over crust. Chill until firm.

10 to 12 servings

AMARETTO PEACH CHEESECAKE ━━━━

3 tablespoons PARKAY
  Margarine
1/3 cup sugar
1 egg
3/4 cup flour
        *   *   *
3 8-oz. pkgs. PHILADELPHIA
  BRAND Cream Cheese,
  softened
3/4 cup sugar
3 tablespoons flour
3 eggs
1 16-oz. can peach halves,
  drained, pureed
1/4 cup almond flavored liqueur

Combine margarine and sugar until light and fluffy. Blend in egg. Add flour; mix well. Spread dough onto bottom of 9-inch springform pan. Bake at 450°, 10 minutes.

Combine cream cheese, sugar and flour, mixing at medium speed on electric mixer until well blended. Add eggs, one at a time, mixing well after each addition. Add peaches and liqueur; mix well. Pour over crust. Bake at 450°, 10 minutes. Reduce oven temperature to 250°; continue baking 65 minutes. Loosen cake from rim of pan; cool before removing rim of pan. Chill. Garnish with peach slices and sliced almonds, toasted, if desired.

10 to 12 servings

CAPPUCCINO CHEESECAKE ━━━━

1 1/2 cups finely chopped nuts
2 tablespoons sugar
3 tablespoons PARKAY
  Margarine, melted
        *   *   *
4 8-oz. pkgs. PHILADELPHIA
  BRAND Cream Cheese,
  softened
1 cup sugar
3 tablespoons flour
4 eggs
1 cup sour cream
1 tablespoon instant coffee
  granules
1/4 teaspoon cinnamon
1/4 cup boiling water

Combine nuts, sugar and margarine; press onto bottom of 9-inch springform pan. Bake at 325°, 10 minutes.

Combine cream cheese, sugar and flour, mixing at medium speed on electric mixer until well blended. Add eggs, one at a time, mixing well after each addition. Blend in sour cream. Dissolve coffee granules and cinnamon in water. Cool; gradually add to cream cheese mixture, mixing until well blended. Pour over crust. Bake at 450°, 10 minutes. Reduce oven temperature to 250°; continue baking 1 hour. Loosen cake from rim of pan; cool before removing rim of pan. Chill. Garnish with whipped cream and whole coffee beans, if desired.

10 to 12 servings

Amaretto Peach Cheesecake

ORANGE UPSIDE-DOWN CHEESECAKE

1 envelope unflavored gelatin
1½ cups KRAFT 100% Pure Unsweetened Orange Juice
¼ cup sugar
2 cups orange sections
        *   *   *
1 envelope unflavored gelatin
½ cup KRAFT 100% Pure Unsweetened Orange Juice
3 8-oz. pkgs. PHILADELPHIA BRAND Cream Cheese, softened
1 cup sugar
2 teaspoons grated orange peel
1 cup whipping cream, whipped
        *   *   *
1 cup vanilla wafer crumbs
½ teaspoon cinnamon
3 tablespoons PARKAY Margarine, melted

Soften gelatin in juice. Add sugar; stir over low heat until dissolved. Chill until slightly thickened. Arrange orange sections on bottom of 9-inch springform pan. Pour gelatin mixture over oranges; chill until thickened but not set.

Soften gelatin in juice; stir over low heat until dissolved. Combine cream cheese, sugar and peel, mixing at medium speed on electric mixer until well blended. Gradually add gelatin mixture, mixing until blended. Chill until slightly thickened; fold in whipped cream. Pour over oranges; chill.

Combine crumbs, cinnamon and margarine; gently press onto top of cake. Chill. Loosen cake from rim of pan; invert onto serving plate.

10 to 12 servings

VARIATION
■ Omit cinnamon. Substitute graham cracker crumbs or chocolate wafer crumbs for vanilla wafer crumbs.

ALOHA CHEESECAKE

1 cup vanilla wafer crumbs
¼ cup PARKAY Margarine, melted
        *   *   *
2 8-oz. pkgs. PHILADELPHIA BRAND Cream Cheese, softened
⅓ cup sugar
2 tablespoons milk
2 eggs
½ cup chopped macadamia nuts, toasted
1 8¼-oz. can crushed pineapple, drained
1 kiwi, peeled, sliced

Combine crumbs and margarine; press onto bottom of 9-inch springform pan. Bake at 350°, 10 minutes.

Combine cream cheese, sugar and milk, mixing at medium speed on electric mixer until well blended. Add eggs, one at a time, mixing well after each addition. Stir in nuts; pour over crust. Bake at 350°, 45 minutes. Loosen cake from rim of pan; cool before removing rim of pan. Chill. Before serving, top with fruit.

10 to 12 servings

Chocolate Chip Cheesecake Supreme

CHOCOLATE CHIP CHEESECAKE SUPREME

1 cup chocolate wafer crumbs
3 tablespoons PARKAY Margarine, melted

*   *   *

3 8-oz. pkgs. PHILADELPHIA BRAND Cream Cheese, softened
3/4 cup sugar
1/4 cup flour
3 eggs
1/2 cup sour cream
1 teaspoon vanilla
1 cup mini semi-sweet chocolate pieces

Combine crumbs and margarine; press onto bottom of 9-inch springform pan. Bake at 350°, 10 minutes.

Combine cream cheese, sugar and flour, mixing at medium speed on electric mixer until well blended. Add eggs, one at a time, mixing well after each addition. Blend in sour cream and vanilla. Stir in chocolate pieces; pour over crust. Bake at 325°, 55 minutes. Loosen cake from rim of pan; cool before removing rim of pan. Chill. Garnish with whipped cream and fresh mint, if desired.

10 to 12 servings

AUTUMN CHEESECAKE

1 cup graham cracker crumbs
3 tablespoons sugar
1/2 teaspoon cinnamon
1/4 cup PARKAY Margarine,
   melted
          *   *   *
2 8-oz. pkgs. PHILADELPHIA
   BRAND Cream Cheese,
   softened
1/2 cup sugar
2 eggs
1/2 teaspoon vanilla
          *   *   *
4 cups thin peeled apple slices
1/3 cup sugar
1/2 teaspoon cinnamon
1/4 cup chopped pecans

Combine crumbs, sugar, cinnamon and margarine; press onto bottom of 9-inch springform pan. Bake at 350°, 10 minutes.

Combine cream cheese and sugar, mixing at medium speed on electric mixer until well blended. Add eggs, one at a time, mixing well after each addition. Blend in vanilla; pour over crust.

Toss apples with combined sugar and cinnamon. Spoon apple mixture over cream cheese layer; sprinkle with pecans. Bake at 350°, 1 hour and 10 minutes. Loosen cake from rim of pan; cool before removing rim of pan. Chill.

10 to 12 servings

VARIATION

■Add 1/2 cup finely chopped pecans with crumbs for crust. Continue as directed.

"PHILLY" CHEESECAKE

1 cup graham cracker crumbs
3 tablespoons PARKAY
   Margarine, melted
          *   *   *
2 8-oz. pkgs. PHILADELPHIA
   BRAND Cream Cheese,
   softened
1/2 cup sugar
1 tablespoon lemon juice
1 teaspoon grated lemon peel
1/2 teaspoon vanilla
2 eggs, separated

Combine crumbs and margarine; press onto bottom of 9-inch springform pan. Bake at 325°, 10 minutes.

Combine cream cheese, sugar, juice, peel and vanilla, mixing at medium speed on electric mixer until well blended. Add egg yolks, one at a time, mixing well after each addition. Fold in stiffly beaten egg whites; pour over crust. Bake at 300°, 45 minutes. Loosen cake from rim of pan; cool before removing rim of pan. Chill. Serve with fresh fruit or cherry pie filling, if desired.

10 to 12 servings

Autumn Cheesecake

PRALINE CHEESECAKE

1 cup graham cracker crumbs
3 tablespoons granulated
 sugar
3 tablespoons PARKAY
 Margarine, melted
 *   *   *
3 8-oz. pkgs. PHILADELPHIA
 BRAND Cream Cheese,
 softened
¾ cup packed dark brown
 sugar
2 tablespoons flour
3 eggs
2 teaspoons vanilla
½ cup finely chopped pecans
 Maple syrup
 Pecan halves

Combine crumbs, granulated sugar and margarine; press onto bottom of 9-inch springform pan. Bake at 350°, 10 minutes.

Combine cream cheese, brown sugar and flour, mixing at medium speed on electric mixer until well blended. Add eggs, one at a time, mixing well after each addition. Blend in vanilla; stir in chopped pecans. Pour over crust. Bake at 450°, 10 minutes. Reduce oven temperature to 250°; continue baking 30 minutes. Loosen cake from rim of pan; cool before removing rim of pan. Chill. Brush with syrup; top with pecan halves.

10 to 12 servings

TEMPTING TRIFLE CHEESECAKE

1½ cups soft coconut macaroon
 cookie crumbs
 *   *   *
3 8-oz. pkgs. PHILADELPHIA
 BRAND Cream Cheese,
 softened
¾ cup sugar
4 eggs
½ cup sour cream
½ cup whipping cream
2 tablespoons sweet sherry
1 teaspoon vanilla
 *   *   *
1 10-oz. jar KRAFT Red
 Raspberry Preserves
½ cup whipping cream,
 whipped
 Toasted slivered almonds

Press crumbs onto bottom of greased 9-inch springform pan. Bake at 325°, 15 minutes.

Combine cream cheese and sugar, mixing at medium speed on electric mixer until well blended. Add eggs, one at a time, mixing well after each addition. Blend in sour cream, whipping cream, sherry and vanilla; pour over crust. Bake at 325°, 1 hour and 10 minutes. Loosen cake from rim of pan; cool before removing rim of pan. Chill.

Heat preserves in saucepan over low heat until melted. Strain to remove seeds. Spoon over cheesecake, spreading to edges. Dollop with whipped cream; top with almonds.

10 to 12 servings

Creamy Chilled Cheesecake

CREAMY CHILLED CHEESECAKE ▬▬▬▬

1 cup graham cracker crumbs
¼ cup sugar
¼ cup PARKAY Margarine, melted

*   *   *

1 envelope unflavored gelatin
¼ cup cold water
1 8-oz. pkg. PHILADELPHIA BRAND Cream Cheese, softened
½ cup sugar
Dash of salt
¾ cup milk
¼ cup lemon juice
1 cup whipping cream, whipped
Strawberry halves

Combine crumbs, sugar and margarine; press onto bottom of 9-inch springform pan.

Soften gelatin in water; stir over low heat until dissolved. Combine cream cheese, sugar and salt, mixing at medium speed on electric mixer until well blended. Gradually add gelatin, milk and juice, mixing until blended. Chill until slightly thickened; fold in whipped cream. Pour over crust; chill until firm. Top with strawberries just before serving.

8 servings

Festive Irish Cream Cheesecake

FESTIVE IRISH CREAM CHEESECAKE

1 cup graham cracker crumbs
¹/₄ cup sugar
¹/₄ cup PARKAY Margarine, melted

*   *   *

1 envelope unflavored gelatin
¹/₂ cup cold water
1 cup sugar
3 eggs, separated
2 8-oz. pkgs. PHILADELPHIA BRAND Cream Cheese, softened
2 tablespoons cocoa
2 tablespoons bourbon
1 cup whipping cream, whipped

Combine crumbs, sugar and margarine; press onto bottom of 9-inch springform pan.

Soften gelatin in water; stir over low heat until dissolved. Blend in ³/₄ cup sugar and beaten egg yolks; cook, stirring constantly, over low heat 3 minutes. Combine cream cheese and cocoa, mixing at medium speed on electric mixer until well blended. Gradually add gelatin mixture and bourbon, mixing until blended. Chill until thickened but not set. Beat egg whites until foamy; gradually add remaining sugar, beating until stiff peaks form. Fold egg whites and whipped cream into cream cheese mixture; pour over crust. Chill until firm. Garnish with chocolate curls and small silver candy balls, if desired.

10 to 12 servings

VARIATION
■ Substitute 2 tablespoons cold coffee for bourbon.

LATTICE CHERRY CHEESECAKE

1 20-oz. pkg. PILLSBURY'S
   BEST Refrigerated Sugar
   Cookies
    *   *   *
2 8-oz. pkgs. PHILADELPHIA
   BRAND Cream Cheese,
   softened
1 cup sour cream
3/4 cup sugar
1/4 teaspoon almond extract
3 eggs
1 21-oz. can cherry pie filling

Freeze cookie dough 1 hour. Slice into 1/8-inch slices. Arrange slices, slightly overlapping, on bottom and sides of greased 9-inch springform pan. With lightly floured fingers, seal edges to form crust.

Combine cream cheese, sour cream, sugar and extract, mixing at medium speed on electric mixer until well blended. Add eggs, one at a time, mixing well after each addition. Reserve 1/4 cup batter; chill. Pour remaining batter over crust. Bake at 350°, 1 hour and 10 minutes. Increase oven temperature to 450°. Spoon pie filling over cheesecake. Spoon reserved batter over pie filling in criss-cross pattern to form lattice design. Bake at 450°, 10 minutes. Loosen cake from rim of pan; cool before removing rim of pan.

10 to 12 servings

VARIATION

■ Substitute 13×9-inch baking pan for 9-inch springform pan. Prepare recipe as directed except for baking. Bake at 350°, 40 minutes. Increase oven temperature to 450°. Continue as directed.

INDEX